More Than Meets the Eye

A Comedy in Three Acts

by Fred Carmichael

A SAMUEL FRENCH ACTING EDITION

FOUNDED 1830
New York Hollywood London Toronto
SAMUELFRENCH.COM

Copyright © 1953 (Under title "The Green Snowman") by Frederick Walker Carmichael
Copyright © 1954 by Samuel French, Inc.
Copyright © 191981, 1982 (in Renewal), by Frederick Walker Carmichael

ALL RIGHTS RESERVED

CAUTION: Professionals and amateurs are hereby warned that *MORE THAN MEETS THE EYE* is subject to a Licensing Fee. It is fully protected under the copyright laws of the United States of America, the British Commonwealth, including Canada, and all other countries of the Copyright Union. All rights, including professional, amateur, motion picture, recitation, lecturing, public reading, radio broadcasting, television and the rights of translation into foreign languages are strictly reserved. In its present form the play is dedicated to the reading public only.

The amateur live stage performance rights to *MORE THAN MEETS THE EYE* are controlled exclusively by Samuel French, Inc., and licensing arrangements and performance licenses must be secured well in advance of presentation. PLEASE NOTE that amateur Licensing Fees are set upon application in accordance with your producing circumstances. When applying for a licensing quotation and a performance license please give us the number of performances intended, dates of production, your seating capacity and admission fee. Licensing Fees are payable one week before the opening performance of the play to Samuel French, Inc., at 45 W. 25th Street, New York, NY 10010.

Licensing Fee of the required amount must be paid whether the play is presented for charity or gain and whether or not admission is charged.

Stock licensing fees quoted upon application to Samuel French, Inc.

For all other rights than those stipulated above, apply to: Samuel French, Inc.

Particular emphasis is laid on the question of amateur or professional readings, permission and terms for which must be secured in writing from Samuel French, Inc.

Copying from this book in whole or in part is strictly forbidden by law, and the right of performance is not transferable.

Whenever the play is produced the following notice must appear on all programs, printing and advertising for the play: "Produced by special arrangement with Samuel French, Inc."

Due authorship credit must be given on all programs, printing and advertising for the play.

No one shall commit or authorize any act or omission by which the copyright of, or the right to copyright, this play may be impaired.
No one shall make any changes in this play for the purpose of production.
Publication of this play does not imply availability for performance. Both amateurs and professionals considering a production are strongly advised in their own interests to apply to Samuel French, Inc., for written permission before starting rehearsals, advertising, or booking a theatre.
No part of this book may be reproduced, stored in a retrieval system, or transmitted in any form, by any means, now known or yet to be invented, including mechanical, electronic, photocopying, recording, videotaping, or otherwise, without the prior written permission of the publisher.

ISBN 978-0-573-61250-3   Printed in U.S.A.   #705

MORE THAN MEETS THE EYE
STORY OF THE PLAY
(5 males; 6 females)

Stanley Nichols, a young author, is taking a year off to write "the great American novel." Unknown to anyone except his immediate family, is the fact that Stanley has written a series of children's stories under the pen name of "Grandma Letty." When he is voted "Grandmother of the Year," reporters, newsreel photographers, and the publisher descend on the quiet Nichols household to meet and interview Grandma. Afraid that, if he is exposed as a juvenile writer, it will hurt his chances for his new novel, Stanley has to produce a Grandma. After all else fails, he impersonates the great lady. Matters get more complicated when the publisher proposes, the reporters suspect a scoop and won't leave, and his wife demands he tell the truth or she will leave him. To help out, Maude, the Nichols' housekeeper, dons the disguise making two Grandmas to confuse the neighbors and reporters. Running through the play is the romance of Stanley's niece, Peggy, who is afraid she is too normal for her overly intelligent boyfriend. When she finally confesses her fears, Bradley points out that "every genius needs a normal woman to keep his feet planted firmly in the family home." In a touching and moving scene, Stanley's wife makes him realize that the solution to his problems lies in the moral of his own books. This comedy is guaranteed to give both audience and actors a wonderful evening in the theatre. Especially recommended to Little Theatre Groups and advanced high school casts.

MORE THAN MEETS THE EYE

(Copy of the program of the first performance of MORE THAN MEETS THE EYE, under title THE GREEN SNOWMAN, presented August 14, 1953, by The Caravan Theatre summer stock company at The Dorset Playhouse, Dorset, Vermont.)

THE GREEN SNOWMAN
by
Fred Carmichael

Staged by Patricia Wyn Rose

Cast (in order of appearance):

MAUDE	Mary Jane Bible
PEGGY	Mary Andrews
NORA	Toni Darryl
CHRISTINE	Katherine Engel
STANLEY	Fred Carmichael
BRADLEY	William Strobbe
PRUDENCE HARPER	Frances Elliott
CARL HENDERSON	Paul McMahon
CYRIL B. HOSKINS	Ward Anderson
MISS JENKINS	Susan Richardson

(The part of Lawton Ellerbe was not in the original production.)

ACT ONE:

The home of Stanley Nichols in a small Midwestern town.

A day this Spring at 11:00 A.M.

SYNOPSIS OF SCENES

ACT TWO:
The same. Immediately afterwards.

ACT THREE:
The same. A short time later.

MORE THAN MEETS THE EYE

DESCRIPTION OF CHARACTERS

STANLEY NICHOLS, *a good looking man in his early thirties. He is about six feet tall, pleasant and happy, although excitable in a crisis. When the play opens, he is tired from working hard and slightly disheveled.*

CHRISTINE NICHOLS *is a few years younger than her husband. Although she seems calm to most observers, she has been living a lie for many years and the toll on her patience is beginning to show. She is very much in love with Stanley and has made him a good wife but, in a showdown, puts her ideals above her husband.*

PEGGY, *a girl in her teens who is quite normal, a little too normal she is afraid. She is not necessarily the sweet ingenue, but more the adolescent growing into young womanhood who, at the moment, is still slightly angular.*

CYRIL B. HOSKINS, *in his sixties or early seventies; he is a man of tremendous vitality. His prime interest in life is his book sales and the publishing firm of Hoskins & Company. At times, he is sentimental but never loses sight of business for an instant.*

NORA, *a housewife slightly older than Christine; she has a good sense of humor that borders on the wry and sarcastic. She is a good friend to the Nichols in spite of the fact that she drops by unannounced several times a day.*

DESCRIPTION OF CHARACTERS

BRADLEY, *a teenager of Peggy's age; he is extremely intelligent without being obnoxiously so. He is pleasant looking despite his serious expression and the glasses he wears.*

PRUDENCE HARPER, *an extremely good looking and sophisticated reporter for LIFE magazine; she is used to barging in where she is not wanted and getting the most out of any situation. She is close to middle age but it is hard to say how old she really is.*

CARL HENDERSON, *a photographer for LIFE magazine; he is never without his camera. He is somewhere in his late thirties and the kind of man who doesn't speak unless it is important. He is not dumb but possibly a little slow to catch onto situations and conversations.*

MISS JENKINS *is the kind of person who takes her job too seriously and forges ahead regardless of the problems that stand in her way. She is in her thirties, attractive in a severe way, and has clear cut and precise speech.*

MAUDE *is, and has been, the housekeeper and cook for Chris' family for years. She is possibly in her fifties and has tremendous loyalty to Chris. She doesn't understand Stanley and doesn't have much patience with him. She is gruff, sometimes curt, but tries very hard to please.*

LAWTON ELLERBE *is a man a great deal like Hoskins, of the same age and temperament.*

More Than Meets The Eye

ACT ONE

The scene of the play is the living room of Stanley Nichols' home in the Midwestern part of the United States. It is a comfortable room slightly on the modern side. Down stage Right is an entrance to the dining room and the kitchen of the house; directly above this is a comfortable armchair with a small table below it. The up stage Right corner of the room contains a double bookcase joined at the corner. On the bottom shelf of the upstage section there are ornaments and bric-a-bric. Below this section of the bookcase there is another chair with a small footstool below it. Up stage from Center to the Left wall and a step up is the entrance hall to the house. Stairs lead off stage to the Right. Below the stairs are a small telephone table and a chair; a window is in the upstage wall: the door to the outside is on the Left wall; a sofa and coffee table are at Left Center. The Left wall is almost completely covered with draperies which pull over French windows. Outside the windows there can be seen the garden of the house.

As the Curtain opens, the front DOORBELL rings. MAUDE enters from the kitchen. She is a middle-aged housekeeper and cook, kindly but with a will of iron. As she is almost to the front door, the PHONE rings. She looks between the two. The PHONE rings again and wins.

ACT I   MORE THAN MEETS THE EYE   9

MAUDE. *(Into phone)* Hello— Yes, she is. Just a minute, please. *(Calls up the stairs)* Peggy. Phone.
PEGGY. *(Off stage upstairs)* Coming.
MAUDE. *(Opens the front door. She reaches around the corner and gets the mail from the box. There are about fifteen letters. Then she leans over and picks up a package. She brings them in, closes the door and starts towards table down Right as* PEGGY *runs down the stairs.)*
PEGGY. *(Is a teen-ager, young and pretty. She is full of life but at the moment has a problem)* Thanks, Maude. *(Into phone)* Hello— Oh, Brad, hi— Sure, I'd love to— Half an hour? I think so. I'll hurry. Just honk for me. *(Slightly aggravated)* All right, come in if you feel you have to. Bye. *(Hangs up. She watches* MAUDE, *who has sorted the mail into two piles and then has crossed to readjust the drapes on the French windows.* PEGGY *is undecided whether to speak or not, then decides in the affirmative)* Maude.
MAUDE. *(Turns)* Yes, Peggy.
PEGGY. *(Leaning on the newel post)* Maude, you've been around a long time.
MAUDE. *(Dryly)* Thanks.
PEGGY. You know what I mean.
MAUDE. *(Smiles at her)* Sure. I know.
PEGGY. So you might be able to answer a question for me.
MAUDE. *(As she starts primping the cushions on the sofa)* What is it?
PEGGY. How do you think a super-intelligent man feels when he finds out he's dating a drip?
MAUDE. What drip? You?
PEGGY. Well—yes.
MAUDE. Why not discuss it with your Aunt and Uncle?
PEGGY. They have enough problems of their own.
MAUDE. Who hasn't?
PEGGY. *(Crossing down into the room)* You may not

realize it, but it's very difficult living with your relatives.

MAUDE. *(Crosses in Center)* Now, you listen to me. You should be real grateful to your Aunt Chris and Uncle Stanley. If it wasn't for them, you'd be living in an orphan's home.

PEGGY. Oh, I am grateful, Maude. It's not that. But they're so young. I can't discuss problems like this with them. I need older, more intelligent advice.

MAUDE. *(Surprised)* From me?

PEGGY. You're the only old person I know.

MAUDE. *(Gives cushion a huge slap and replaces it)* O.K. I'll be your Dorothy Dix. What's the problem?

PEGGY. *(Nervously pacing up above chair Right Center)* I've been dating Bradley quite steadily.

MAUDE. I gathered that.

PEGGY. *(Crosses by chair down Right)* I like him and I think he likes me, too. We see eye to eye in almost everything.

MAUDE. Then what's troubling you?

PEGGY. *(Stops moving)* Well, there's an insurmountable difference between us. When he discovers it, then what?

MAUDE. What's this insurmountable thing?

PEGGY. The fact is that he's a genius. What's going to happen when he finds out I'm so dumb?

MAUDE. *(Crosses to Left of* PEGGY*)* What are you talking about? You're not dumb.

PEGGY. *(Sits facing* MAUDE*)* Not really stupid, maybe, but I'm not in Brad's class. Why, he even stumps the teachers at school. "A budding Einstein," that's what they call him. So far, I've managed to keep him off deep subjects, but the time is coming when he'll stump me and I know it. Why, the other day he started arguing about the Pythagorean Theorem.

MAUDE. What did you do?

PEGGY. *(Bashfully)* I sneezed.

MAUDE. *(Crosses back to sofa)* You're not dumb.

PEGGY. *(Rises and crosses Center)* By the time I

recovered, he'd forgotten what he was saying. But I can't keep on sneezing all through every date, can I?

MAUDE. *(As she wipes out the ash tray on the coffee table)* Don't you think he likes you for yourself?

PEGGY. *(Sits Right arm of sofa)* He likes me because I'm a philosopher's niece. He thinks I'm like Stan.

MAUDE. Where did he get the idea your uncle was a philosopher?

PEGGY. *(As she flops backwards onto the sofa)* I told him.

MAUDE. Well, he isn't—not by a long shot.

PEGGY. But this new book will establish him.

MAUDE. It stinks.

PEGGY. What an awful thing to say. It's wonderful.

MAUDE. Have you read it?

PEGGY. Well—no.

MAUDE. I have.

PEGGY. *(Surprised, she swings her feet onto the floor and sits up)* You have—when?

MAUDE. One night he left the manuscript down here and I took it upstairs to bed with me. Put me to sleep.

PEGGY. You just didn't understand it—that's all.

MAUDE. I understood it all right. That was the trouble.

PEGGY. Just wait and you'll see. Stan will be famous one day.

MAUDE. *(Points to the package that came in the mail)* He is now.

PEGGY. In a way—maybe.

MAUDE. Wait until your Bradley finds out that Stan is—

PEGGY. *(Jumping up)* Maude! Never, never say that. You promised.

MAUDE. *(Crosses below the coffee table to Right Center)* But he'll find out sometime. Everyone will.

PEGGY. Why should they? They haven't yet.

MAUDE. You can't keep something like that quiet even if you do move way out here in the wilderness.

PEGGY. This isn't the wilderness—it's a very nice town.
MAUDE. All the same, they'll find out—mark my words.
PEGGY. If Brad knew, he'd never forgive Stan—he wouldn't even take me out any more—it would ruin us.
MAUDE. If Bradley goes out with you just for what your uncle is, then all I can say is, he ain't worth much.
PEGGY. It isn't that. He thinks I'm as smart as Stan is.
MAUDE. That's where I came in. I'd better go back to work and you'd better go on sneezing.
PEGGY. I'm all sneezed out. *(Turns upstage to back of sofa.)*

(NORA RAMSON *enters through the French windows. She is the next door neighbor and like many others of the species, she drops in several times during the usual day. She is about 30, fairly attractive and has a keen, but dry, sense of humor.)*

MAUDE. Mornin', Mrs. Ramson.
NORA. Hello, Maude— Peggy.
PEGGY. *(Sadly)* Hi, Nora.
NORA. *(Crosses to front of sofa)* Chris not up yet?
PEGGY. She's around somewhere.
MAUDE. Upstairs. *(Menacingly at* NORA*)* Did she ask you here for coffee?
NORA. Sure did.
MAUDE. She never told *me!*
NORA. She did ask me. Cross my heart.
MAUDE. *(Furious, almost shouting at* NORA*)* Then you'd better sit down!
NORA. *(Sits, surprised)* Thanks.
MAUDE. *(As she exits into kitchen mumbling)* Doesn't tell me. Never tells me anything. Thinks I'm a mind reader. *(She slams the door behind her.)*
NORA. *(Laughs)* Now I've done it.

ACT I MORE THAN MEETS THE EYE

PEGGY. *(Crosses and sits in stool up Right)* She doesn't approve of Chris asking people without telling her.

NORA. Is she really angry?

PEGGY. *(Shaking her head)* She'll make instant coffee and not talk for an hour or so. Then it will all blow over.

NORA. As long as she doesn't quit. Servants are hard to come by these days.

PEGGY. Maude wouldn't leave—she's part of the family. She even keeps a scrapbook of all of us including one of Chris on a bearskin rug.

NORA. None of Stanley?

PEGGY. He didn't come into the picture until Chris hooked him.

NORA. How is the author these days—book coming along well?

PEGGY. Fine— I hope. He's always working on it.

NORA. *(Yawns as she tucks her feet under her)* Ambitious man, your uncle. I never understood how anyone could concentrate long enough to write a book.

PEGGY. He seems to enjoy it.

NORA. And such a deep book, too. He told me it's going to be another *War and Peace* only with more of a message.

CHRIS. *(Off stage upstairs calling)* Is that you, Nora?

NORA. It's me.

CHRIS. *(Upstairs)* Be right down. I have a surprise for you.

NORA. All right. *(To PEGGY)* What's Chris up to?

PEGGY. Who knows? *(Looks at her wristwatch)* But I'm up to a date and quick. *(Starts to run up the stairs)* See you later. *(Stops and turns)* Nora, do you think I'm intelligent?

NORA. I should say you're normal. Why?

PEGGY. Normal isn't good enough. I've just got to be a genius. *(She exits. From off stage, we hear her voice)* Chris, what on earth are you doing like that?

CHRIS. *(Off stage)* It's for Saturday night.
PEGGY. *(As her voice fades away)* You look hysterical.
NORA. What's going on up there?
CHRIS. Ready, Nora?
NORA. Ready for what? *(She twists on the sofa to watch CHRIS come downstairs.)*

(CHRIS *comes down the stairs. She is an attractive woman in her late twenties, intelligent, sincere, and the type who fits into any group and who gets along well with everyone. At the moment she presents a rather bizarre sight. She is dressed as an old lady. On her head is a grey wig, soft waves in front and a large bun at the back. She wears a skirt which is too large and too long for her, and over her shoulders is a brightly colored scarf with fringe hanging from it. She wears silver rimmed glasses. As she comes down the stairs she is humming "Little Old Lady.")*

NORA. *(As she and CHRIS laugh)* Chris, you look marvelous.
CHRIS. *(She lifts the wig and peers out from under it)* Guess who?
NORA. That's not what you're going to wear?
CHRIS. Why not? The invitation said, "Come dressed as your ambition."
NORA. And that's yours?
CHRIS. I'm going to end up an old lady so why not want to be one, that's my philosophy. *(She takes off the costume, putting the skirt, shawl, and glasses on the telephone table and the wig over the phone.)*
NORA. It doesn't fit too well.
CHRIS. I know. I have to take up the hem and nip it in here and **there**.
NORA. *(Making an Egyptian gesture with her hands)* I'm going as Cleopatra.
CHRIS. What's Bert going as?

ACT I   MORE THAN MEETS THE EYE

NORA. The asp!
CHRIS. *(Laughs)* I think my husband's dressing as Socrates. He should at the rate the book's going.
NORA. See much of him these days?
CHRIS. For a young married couple supposedly cruising through love's young dream, we might fail the test, but we do speak at dinner. *(She sits in chair up Right Center with her knitting which was in chair.)*
NORA. It had better be a good book.
CHRIS. You can say that twice.
NORA. It had better—
CHRIS. I take it back. Once is enough.
NORA. Knitting something for Stan?
CHRIS. No, this time it's for me. A sweater.
NORA. Smart girl. That ought to get his attention.
CHRIS. If I ever get through the ribbing, it's going to be striped.

(The kitchen door opens and MAUDE enters with two cups of coffee on a tray. She crosses to the coffee table, puts the tray down with something of a bang and turns to go.)

CHRIS. *(Finally realizing what is the matter)* Maude, I forgot to tell you Nora was coming, didn't I?
MAUDE. *(Still angry)* Uh-huh!
CHRIS. *(Holding up her knitting)* I was so—busy.
MAUDE. Uh-huh!
CHRIS. *(Tentatively)* I'm sorry.
MAUDE. Uh-huh!
CHRIS. Thanks for bringing it in.
MAUDE. *(As she exits)* Uh-huh!
CHRIS. *(Turns to NORA)* Been with us for generations.
NORA. Uh-huh!
CHRIS. Taught me everything when I was a girl.

(The kitchen door opens and MAUDE pokes her head back in and points to the table down Right.)

MAUDE. Mail! *(Closes the door again.)*
CHRIS. *(As she crosses to the mail)* She gets moments of extreme talkativeness. This just doesn't happen to be one of them.
NORA. You'd better open the mail or she'll quit.
CHRIS. Help yourself to the coffee. Mine black as usual. *(She starts to open the mail.)*
STAN. *(Calling from upstairs)* Chris!
CHRIS. Yes, dear.
STAN. *(Upstairs)* Coffee!
CHRIS. *(To NORA)* Another loquacious creature, my husband.
STAN. *(Upstairs)* Huh?
CHRIS. Nothing, dear. One black coming up. *(Calling toward kitchen)* Maude.
NORA. I predict a monosyllabic answer.
MAUDE. *(Enters from kitchen)* Yes.

(CHRIS *and* NORA *turn to her.*)

NORA. *(As CHRIS turns and smiles at her)* Call me swami.
CHRIS. *(To MAUDE)* Maude, Mr. Nichols wants some coffee, too.
MAUDE. Oh. *(She exits.)*
NORA. We'd better have coffee at my place tomorrow.
CHRIS. *(As she resumes opening mail)* But you're two cups ahead of me already.
NORA. Three, but who's counting.
CHRIS. *(Starts to read a letter)* Wait until his lord and master gets this. *(She laughs.)*
NORA. What is it?
CHRIS. *(Feeling guilty)* Oh, nothing much. Just a bill.
NORA. Do you always laugh at bills? *(Crosses with* CHRIS' *coffee)* Let's see.
CHRIS. No. You wouldn't be interested.
NORA. You always get so much mail. *(Tries to look*

at letter but CHRIS *puts it back in the envelope)* Do you enter contests or something?

CHRIS. *(Takes coffee and puts it on table Right)* Just ads. *(She undoes the package and then tries to hide the contents.)*

NORA. Let me see.

CHRIS. *(Hiding them behind her)* Just some books?

NORA. What's the matter—are they dirty?

CHRIS. Of course not.

NORA. Well, then, let's look. *(Takes the books from* CHRIS. *Crosses up stage)* Really, Mrs. Nichols, at your age.

CHRIS. They're cute.

NORA. *(Reading the title)* "Grandma Letty and the Green Snowman."

CHRIS. Awfully cute. *(She laughs weakly.)*

MAUDE. *(Enters with coffee cup and saucer. As she crosses below* NORA *who is in her way)* Pardon. *(She starts upstairs.)*

NORA. Certainly.

MAUDE. Coffee. *(She exits upstairs.)*

NORA. That girl needs Lydia Pinkham's.

CHRIS. Give me the books, Nora.

NORA. *(Looking through them)* They're all the same.

CHRIS. I know it. They're—birthday presents.

NORA. For whom?

CHRIS. Oh, nieces and nephews and things.

NORA. Not Peggy, I hope.

CHRIS. No, but she's read most of Grandma Letty's books.

NORA. Really?

CHRIS. Yes, they're good.

NORA. Everywhere you look nowadays, it's Grandma Letty. She must put out a book a month.

CHRIS. They're very well written children's books with a good moral.

NORA. The old girl must be coining a fortune.

CHRIS. She deserves it. Have you ever read one?

NORA. *(Hands books back to* CHRIS *and crosses*

Left) I'll wait until Grandma Letty Meets Frankenstein and I'll bet the monster runs from Granny.

CHRIS. *(Crossing up stage slightly)* They're the biggest selling juvenile books since the Oz series.

MAUDE. *(As she comes down the stairs, NORA is again in her way)* Pardon again.

NORA. Certainly again.

MAUDE. Thank you. *(She exits into the kitchen.)*

CHRIS. Two words. She won't be angry much longer.

NORA. *(Sits on the sofa and sips her coffee)* I didn't know you had so many relatives.

CHRIS. *(Takes books and knitting to stool by Right chair)* Birthday's pile up—and Easter.

NORA. All right. Don't tell me. But if *I* get one for Christmas, we're through. No more coffee.

CHRIS. I'll give you "Lady Chatterly's Lover."

NORA. I read it when I was eight.

CHRIS. I don't doubt it.

(They BOTH *laugh.* STANLEY *hurries down the stairs. He is a good-looking man in his early thirties. He has been working late the night before and all morning so looks tired at the moment. He wears a sports shirt and slacks. He is very preoccupied and stops a few steps from the bottom.)*

STAN. Chris, I— Oh, hello Nora.

NORA. Hi, W. Somerset.

STAN. *(After a look at* NORA*)* Did you get any more typing paper?

CHRIS. Right there on the telephone table.

STAN. *(Reaches over the bannister and picks it up)* Thanks. What's the matter with Maude; she angry at something?

CHRIS. I didn't tell her Nora was coming for coffee.

STAN. Oh, that all. *(He runs upstairs.)*

NORA. There goes the busiest man on this block.

CHRIS. There goes the nicest man on any block.

NORA. Seriously, Chris, how is the book coming?

CHRIS. He's almost through the final revision.
NORA. Have you read it yet?
CHRIS. The first half.
NORA. It's a real drama, isn't it?
CHRIS. Yes. Definitely.
NORA. That's what I was afraid of. Why does everybody write tragedies? It seems to me people want to laugh.
CHRIS. This is Stan's one big fling as he calls it. His sabbatical to write the great American novel.
NORA. Then back to pulp magazines?
CHRIS. If the book doesn't sell.
NORA. *(Her curiosity almost getting the better of her)* But with no money coming in—
CHRIS. There's still the inheritance from his grandfather.
NORA. It must be a big one. You two have been here almost a year now and with all that outgo and no income, it's enough to strain any inheritance.
CHRIS. We'll manage.
MAUDE. *(Enters from kitchen armed with a mop, dustpan, and broom)* Excuse me, I gotta finish cleaning Peggy's room.
CHRIS. *(As* MAUDE *crosses to the foot of the stairs)* All right, but do it quietly. Mr. Nichols is working.
MAUDE. *(Poses with broom pointed up the stairs as if it were a spear)* Dust waits for no man. *(She charges up the stairs.)*
CHRIS. *(Rises and crosses to the bottom shelf of the bookcase for knitting magazine)* She thinks that's from Shakespeare.
NORA. Any time your better half wants peace and quiet, you know you're always welcome next door.
CHRIS. If he throws me out, I'll remember that.
NORA. That goes for Maude and Peggy, too.
CHRIS. Peggy would just move over to Brad's, I'm afraid.
NORA. I'm glad those two are getting along so well.

CHRIS. They make a nice couple. Peggy's fitted in well here, hasn't she?

NORA. It must have been a hard adjustment for her to make after her parents were killed.

CHRIS. Jane would be proud of her, the way she's grown up.

NORA. It was nice of Stan to let you bring Peggy into the family.

CHRIS. He suggested it right after the accident. They get along beautifully. Moving out here helped, I think. No memories in a new town.

(There is a loud CRASH from upstairs: possibly that of a chair falling over.)

PEGGY. *(Upstairs)* Maude, for Pete's sake!

CHRIS. Oh—oh.

STAN. *(Upstairs speaking almost simultaneously with PEGGY)* My God, what happened?

MAUDE. *(Upstairs)* Dropped a chair.

STAN. *(Upstairs)* How can I work with all this going on. Chris!

CHRIS. *(Crossing to foot of stairs)* Yes, dear.

NORA. *(Rises)* I'd better go.

CHRIS. Maybe you should.

NORA *(As she hastily exits through French windows)* See you later.

CHRIS. *(Calling after her)* I'll phone you.

STAN. *(Comes downstairs. He is very annoyed)* Chris. what is this conspiracy to keep me from concentrating?

CHRIS. "Dust waits for no man." Maude's got to clean.

STAN. She isn't cleaning. She's wrecking the house room by room. *(He pulls a package of cigarettes from his pocket and takes out the last one.)*

CHRIS. We're not going to live in a dust heap. *(Pushes him onto the sofa)* So you take a minute off and relax. Read the mail. *(She crosses and gets letters and books as* STAN *lights his cigarette.)*

STAN. Just one minute off though. I'm doing well this morning.

CHRIS. That's good *(She crosses to him above the sofa)* Look, here's the new book.

STAN. *(Leafs through it quickly)* Looks fine. Should make a lot of money for Grandma Letty.

CHRIS. *(Leaning over his shoulder with her arms around him)* Don't be that way, honey. I think it's wonderful. Look at the illustrations—better than ever.

STAN. Let me see the mail. *(Takes it from her.)*

CHRIS. *(Crosses up Left of sofa)* Honestly, Stanley, I wish you would take an interest in the books and feel as proud of them as I do. Think of the thousands of children they give fun to.

STAN. Let's not begin that all over again.

MAUDE. *(Comes down the stairs empty handed)* I've given up. Her highness is dressing for a date with I.Q. There's no use cleaning while she's putting on her face.

CHRIS. It's all right, Maude. Brad's picking her up soon.

MAUDE. Good. *(She starts to exit to kitchen.)*

CHRIS. You can finish up later.

MAUDE. *(Turns to* STANLEY. *Fiendishly)* Resting up awhile, Grandma Letty? *(She exits.)*

STAN. *(Rises and stamps out cigarette on coffee table ash tray)* Christine, I will not have her talk that way. I don't care if she did change your diapers.

CHRIS. She doesn't mean any harm.

STAN. That's not the point. *(He crosses Center and turns)* Suppose someone heard her call me Grandma Letty? We'd be through—laughed out of town.

CHRIS. *(Crosses in below sofa)* Why? They'd only respect you.

STAN. *(Crosses down Right)* Respect a grownup man writing kid's books under the name of Grandma Letty? Ha!

CHRIS. Who cares what name you write under? The

books are good, darned good, and I'm proud of them.

STAN. You just wait until the new one is published under my own name. Then I'll forget Grandma Letty and—

CHRIS. Stanley, you can't stop writing them. I don't care if the masterpiece *is* a masterpiece. *(Holding up the book)* These are important.

STAN. Wait a minute. Remember the bargain— I have one year.

CHRIS. *(Drops the book on the coffee table and sits)* Which is almost up.

STAN. One year to write my new book. If it doesn't come off, then we'll go back to "Grandma Letty and the Sweet Smelling Skunk." But no arguments until the end of the year.

CHRIS. All right. But I'm tired of lying to all the neighbors. We live off your grandfather's inheritance indeed. He didn't leave anything but bills and an unfinished subscription to *Esquire*.

STAN. *(Smiling in spite of himself)* That's not kind. *(Crosses towards* CHRIS*)* We have to explain our income somehow.

CHRIS. Just now, Nora asked me why we get so much mail and why we got five Grandma Letty books this morning. I'm tired of thinking one step ahead of everyone else.

STAN. One step ahead of Nora is still behind.

CHRIS. Stanley, Nora's been wonderful to us—the whole town has.

STAN. *(Sits beside her on the sofa and takes her in his arms)* I know it and I'm sorry, honey. I'm just upset about the revisions. I guess I've been working too hard. *(Kisses her)* Forgive me?

(The DOORBELL rings.)

CHRIS. *(Calling towards kitchen)* I'll get it, Maude.
STAN. What a time to be interrupted.

CHRIS. *(As she crosses toward the front door, smiling)* I'll still be around. *(She opens the door)*
    (BRADLEY stands there. He is a young boy the same age as PEGGY. As PEGGY has said, he is intelligent and knows it, but he is very unobtrusive and not at all conceited. He wears slacks, a sport jacket, and glasses.)
Bradley, come in and I'll call Peggy.
    BRAD. Thank you, Mrs. Nichols. *(He closes the door as CHRIS goes upstairs)* Hi, Mr. Nichols.
    STAN. Hello, Brad. Sit down.
    BRAD. *(As he sits on the edge of the chair up Right)* Thank you, sir.
    STAN. Off to a movie? *(STAN starts looking through the mail.)*
    BRAD. No, sir. Just a coke. It's eleven-thirty in the morning, sir.
    STAN. *(Glances at his watch and puts down the mail)* Oh, so it is. Well, you can have a coke here.
    BRAD. Thank you, sir, but you have to ask a girl out occasionally, don't you?
    STAN. Yes, I guess you do.
    BRAD. Girls think it's peculiar if you just want to take them for a walk. They think you ought to buy them something. It's the end of the month and my allowance is running out. That's why we're going out for a coke.
    STAN. *(Laughing)* You've got it all figured out, haven't you?
    BRAD. On paper. *(Gets a small notebook from his coat pocket)* It's figured in my budget. You see, on my allowance, once a week I can afford to take Peggy to a movie with all the trimmings.
    STAN. Trimmings?
    BRAD. *(Surprised he doesn't understand)* Popcorn during, banana split after.
    STAN. *(Smiling)* I see.
    BRAD. That leaves two extra cash dates a month with an occasional coke now and then.

STAN. And this is an occasional date?
BRAD. That's right. Allowance comes in next week and then I begin all over again.
STAN. I never figured dating quite that way.
BRAD. We have to be practical in this day and age, don't we, sir?
STAN. I've just been trying to explain the same thing to my wife.
BRAD. I don't think women understand the financial side of life, do you, sir?
STAN. I doubt it and stop calling me "sir." I'm not ancient.
BRAD. Just a mark of respect to your intelligence, sir.
STAN. Well, that's a new one. What makes you think I'm intelligent?
BRAD. You're a writer and a philosopher.
STAN. I *was* a writer, yes for— *(Puts the top Grandma Letty book upside down on the others)* —for —pulp magazines. As for being a philosopher—well, everyone has a philosophy and being an author, I write mine down, that's all. So more "sirs."
BRAD. No, sir. I mean, "No."
STAN. That's better.
PEGGY. *(Comes downstairs)* Hi.
BRAD. *(Bounces up when he sees* PEGGY. *Crosses up to door and opens it)* Hi, Peggy. All ready?
PEGGY. Uh-huh. Bye, Stan. See you later.
STAN. Don't drink too much.
BRAD. Not on an occasional date.
PEGGY. What's that mean?
STAN. Something practical you wouldn't understand.
BRAD. *(To* PEGGY) Come on. I've got a new book I want you to read. It's on the origin of existentialism.
PEGGY. Huh?
BRAD. Existentialism.
   (PEGGY *sneezes violently.*)
Gesundheit!
STAN. Getting a cold?

ACT I   MORE THAN MEETS THE EYE   25

PEGGY. No. Just a tickle in my nose.
BRAD. Let's go. Good-bye, Mr. Nichols.
STAN. So long. *(Returns to the mail.)*
BRAD. *(As they go out the door)* As I started to say, do you think existentialism is here to stay?

(A violent sneeze from PEGGY as the door closes.)

CHRIS. *(As she comes down the stairs)* Was that Peggy sneezing?
STAN. Yes, a tickle in the nose.
CHRIS. *(Coming into the room)* She must be allergic to Bradley. Whenever he takes her out, she always sneezes.
STAN. People can't be allergic to other people.
CHRIS. Why not? You're allergic to roses so why can't Peggy be allergic to Bradley?
STAN. It just doesn't work that way.
CHRIS. Maybe you're right, but there must be some reason. Did you finish the mail?
STAN. Not yet. *(As he starts opening mail)* It's a good thing I got Hoskins to address the mail to me and not to Grandma Letty.
CHRIS. *(Sits on the Right arm of the sofa)* Why?
STAN. Postmen are awful gossips.
CHRIS. Can't get any dirt out of ours. You know it's a wonder Hoskins has never found out about you. Imagine a publisher never meeting one of his best authors.
STAN. I told him that's the way Grandma wanted it—said she was a shy, retiring soul.
CHRIS. *(Picking out the letter she read earlier)* Read this one. I saved it especially.
STAN. *(Lies back on the sofa with his head in CHRIS' lap. Reading)* "We, the makers of Creamy Dove, the all-purpose shortening, would like to have a debate on our program between Grandma Letty and Grandma Moses on old-fashioned pie-making."

CHRIS. *(Laughing)* I can just see you making a pie on TV.

STAN. Simple. Just add water and roll. *(Opens the next letter)* I'd better answer that and give them the usual, bashful reply. *(Reading)* "Dear Grandma Letty. My little girl won't stop throwing stones at her playmates. A note from you would fix this naughty habit, I'm sure. She idolizes you as does all young America."

CHRIS. That's nice, isn't it?

STAN. Take a letter, Mrs. Nichols. "Dear Stone-Thrower, For better results, suggest you use sling-shot. Love, Grandma Letty." *(He starts to rip up the letter.)*

CHRIS. *(Stopping him and taking the letter from him)* Stanley, you save that letter and answer it nicely.

STAN. *(Sits up)* I get so many of them. It takes me a full day a week to get caught up on the mail alone.

CHRIS. But it makes you feel good knowing you're helping all those little children, doesn't it?

STAN. *(Trying to convince himself, too)* It does not.

CHRIS. I know you, Mr. Nichols. You're lying.

STAN. I am not.

CHRIS. *(Pulling his face around to hers)* You are, too.

STAN. *(Smiling)* Well, maybe a little.

CHRIS. *(Shoves him away gently)* A lot.

STAN. Suppose I am. What good does it do to write one little girl in— *(Picks up the letter)* —East Underlake, Idaho, not to throw stones?

CHRIS. Multiply it by the thousands of letters you write and it does a *lot* of good.

STAN. *(He takes CHRIS' hand in his)* Just wait until my new book is out. It will reach everyone at once and teach them to think for themselves. That's the trouble with people, Chris, they get pushed along with the tide. They get dragged into things by advertising, by public opinion, by keeping up with the Joneses. If only people would think for themselves once in awhile, the whole world would be a lot better off.

CHRIS. *(Stroking his hair)* Of course, darling, but

you're not a one-man crusade out to save the universe single-handed. Sure, write your book, but write Grandma Letty too. Let the whole world know you can do both. Write for all ages.

STAN. *(Rises and crosses to table down Right for cigarette)* Fat chance people would take me seriously if they knew I wrote about cabbage patches in the morning and the meaning of life in the afternoon.

CHRIS. *(Quietly)* It's your talent. I hope you know what you're doing with it.

STAN. It's our talent, Chris, and I do know. As long as Grandma can tide us through financially, O.K., but she's got to be a well locked up skeleton in our closet.

(DOORBELL rings.)

CHRIS. *(As she goes to the door)* Now what?

STAN. I'd better put the books away. *(He picks them up from the coffee table and puts them on the bottom shelf of the bookcase with the title inside.)*

CHRIS. *(From outside the door)* Thank you. *(She comes in and closes the door)* It's a telegram. Must be from Hoskins. It's addressed to G. L., care of Stanley Nichols.

STAN. Let me see. *(Crosses to* CHRIS *up Center. He opens it and reads it)* Oh, no! No! It couldn't be. Chris, what'll we do?

CHRIS. What is it?

STAN. He can't!

CHRIS. Give it to me. *(She reads aloud while* STANLEY *stands, still struck dumb)* "You have been chosen Grandmother of the Year. Arriving on afternoon train to present you with plaque." Oh, Stan. "Forgive intrusion, but you are a national figure and cannot remain in seclusion. Cyril B. Hoskins."

STAN. *(Outraged)* They have no right electing me Grandmother of the Year without my permission.

CHRIS. It's an honor.

STAN. Not to me.

CHRIS. Now you'll *have* to tell Hoskins the truth.

STAN. *(Takes telegram and paces up and down)* No. Say Grandma's out. Gone to India. Swallowed her knitting needle. Say anything.

CHRIS. You'll have to face it. Hoskins will find out.

STAN. He mustn't. What will happen to our income? I can see the papers. *(Gesturing an imaginary headline)* "Grandma Letty A Young Man. Not even a Father."

CHRIS. Couldn't you just take the plaque and say, "Thanks. We'll give it to her when she comes in"?

STAN. Fat chance. He'll want some photographs from the old family album. This will raise book sales three hundrd per cent. *(Turning front)* Think of it—me, Grandmother of the Year.

CHRIS. You'd better learn to bake those pies.

STAN. There's no need to get excited. *(Crosses to sofa)* Let's sit down and be calm—everyone in this room.

CHRIS. *(Looking around)* All two of us?

STAN. Yes, all two.

(They BOTH *sit on the sofa.)*

CHRIS. *(After a pause)* What now, Grandma?

STAN. I'm thinking. *(He rises and crosses to the French windows. Turns and starts to speak)* No. *(He crosses up to the hallway. Gets an idea, turns)*

(CHRIS *looks at him.*)

(He thinks better of it and gives up) Hoskins has to meet Grandma, even for a minute. He has to.

CHRIS. He can't.

STAN. He must. Where can we find a Grandma Letty?

(MAUDE *enters from the kitchen on her way upstairs to finish cleaning.* STAN *stares at her. Then at* CHRIS. *Back at* MAUDE *again. She stops dead in her tracks.*

He points at her menacingly. She looks behind her.)

MAUDE. Are you pointing at me?
CHRIS. No, Stan. She won't do.
STAN. *(Slowly advancing toward* MAUDE*)* She'll have to do. *(Puts his arm around* MAUDE, *a wicked gleam is in his eye)* Maude. Dear Maude. Come and sit down. *(Pushes her towards chair up Right.)*
MAUDE. What's the matter?
STAN. Nothing. Nothing at all. *(Sits her)* Everything's wonderful now that you're here.
MAUDE. Miss Christine—help!
CHRIS. *(Rises and crosses in Left)* I'm trying, Maude. Stan, it wouldn't work.
STAN. It's got to work.
MAUDE. Do I work it?
STAN. You're it.
MAUDE. I'm what?
STAN. You're Grandma Letty.
MAUDE. I am!
STAN. Listen. *(He kneels by her chair)* Cyril B. Hoskins, Grandma's publisher, is coming here this afternoon. Grandma has been voted Grandmother of the Year and he has to give her a plaque.

(MAUDE *starts to laugh and* STAN *tries to drown her out.)*

He has to see her for just a little while.
MAUDE. *(Continues laughing until she realizes the plot)* And I'm what he sees?
STAN. That's right.
MAUDE. *(Rises)* Oh, no!
STAN. *(Pushes her back into the chair. Desperately)* Do you want that nice large salary of yours to stop?
MAUDE. No, sir.
STAN. Then just let Mr. Hoskins see you for one minute. Besides, think of all the children who believe there *is* a Grandma Letty. You can't let them down.
MAUDE. Just one minute, huh?

STAN. That's right. All you have to do is take the plaque, thank him, and leave the rest up to me. We'll give you all day tomorrow off.

(He looks to CHRIS *for agreement and she nods.)*

MAUDE. *(Thinking it over)* I was a good actress in my day. Played Topsy in high school.
STAN. Will you, Maude? Please?
MAUDE. Well—all right. If I get off tomorrow before breakfast.
CHRIS. I'll scramble the eggs.
MAUDE. But I don't look like a sweet old grandmother.
STAN. No, you don't. *(He turns upstage and sees the costume* CHRIS *has left)* The costume! *(He crosses to it.)*
CHRIS. It won't fit. I have to take up the hem.
STAN. It'll have to do. *(Crosses back with costume)* Here, Maude. This will make you look perfect.
MAUDE. I'd better try it on.
CHRIS. *(Takes* MAUDE *by the hand)* Come on up to my room. There's a full length mirror there. *(Picks up the knitting.)*
STAN. *(Takes the wig from over the phone)* I'm coming, too. You need rehearsal.
MAUDE. *(On stairs)* I don't approve, but if it's to save lots of little children from being disillusioned, I'll do it.
STAN. *(As the three of them disappear upstairs)* That's right. This is the most important meeting since the Lone Ranger first saw Silver.

(There is a pause. PRUDENCE HARPER *comes in through the French windows. She is a very attractive woman in her middle thirties. She gives the appearance of being cynical, cold, and very sophisticated, but underneath she is warm and even sentimental. She is dressed strikingly and very fashion-*

ably. Seeing no one is in the room, she signals out the French windows for someone else to come in. CARL HENDERSON *enters. He is about forty, short and tending to overweight. Although not too bright, he knows his business and is good at it. Never without his camera, it now hangs around his neck.)*

PRUDENCE. Come on, Tenderfoot, it's safe. *(She crosses to the kitchen door and peers in.)*

CARL. I still don't approve. Why don't we come in through the front door like normal people?

PRUDENCE. *(On her way to look up the stairs)* Because I'm a reporter and you're a photographer. We're not normal.

CARL. *(Still nervous)* Just the same, it isn't right. We could be arrested for illegal entry.

PRUDENCE. *Life Magazine* would get us off all right. They have influence.

CARL. I wish you would have phoned for an appointment.

PRUDENCE. A surprise attack, darling, is a half-won battle.

CARL. *(Looking around)* No one seems surprised.

PRUDENCE. *(Crossing to Center)* Just let me look around. You can never tell what someone like me might find.

CARL. *(Sits on the sofa)* Go ahead, but don't take anything.

PRUDENCE. I'm not a souvenir hunter.

CARL. Things look normal enough.

PRUDENCE. Not to me.

CARL. What do you mean? Did you find something?

PRUDENCE. Look around you, Sherlock. Don't you notice anything?

CARL. Such as?

PRUDENCE. This doesn't look like an old woman's house.

CARL. Doesn't it?

PRUDENCE. *(Sits on the edge of the coffee table facing* CARL*)* No. Where's the lavendar and old lace? Where's the crocheted afghan on the sofa? Where are the pictures of the imbecilic grandchildren?

CARL. You mean maybe she isn't such a typical grandmother?

PRUDENCE. *(Rises and crosses to above Left end of sofa)* Maybe not. What a story it would make. Grandma Letty drinks three martinis before dinner.

CARL. But what do I take pictures of?

PRUDENCE. Wait awhile. Let's look around first. There must be *some* dark secrets here. Everyone has them.

CARL. But I thought she was such a sweet old lady.

PRUDENCE. Why?

CARL. Well—she's a grandmother.

PRUDENCE. Have you ever seen her?

CARL. You know I haven't.

PRUDENCE. Neither have I. *(Crosses Center)* Listen, darling, from the way Hoskins acted yesterday, I don't think he has either. That's why I persuaded *Life* to send us down here. If a publisher hasn't met one of his best authors, there's a reason.

CARL. You mean, maybe Grandma ain't a grandma, she's a floozie?

PRUDENCE. I don't know, but just because she writes sweet little stories doesn't mean she sits home and crochets antimacassars. Here she is Grandmother of the Year and no one knows anything about her.

(A burst of LAUGHTER comes from upstairs.)

STAN. *(Upstairs)* Hold still, Maude.

MAUDE. *(Upstairs)* But it don't look right.

CHRIS. *(Upstairs)* What a Grandma!

PRUDENCE. *(At foot of stairs looking up)* It must be she—the old girl.

CARL. What did she mean—it don't look right?

PRUDENCE. I don't know.

(NORA *appears at the French windows.*)

CARL. *(Sees* NORA*)* Pru, we got company.

PRUDENCE. *(Turns and sees* NORA. *Here is a conquest and someone who might be helpful, so she gushes accordingly, hardly stopping to take a breath)* Why, you must be Mrs. Nichols. I'm Prudence Harper of *Life Magazine* and this is my photographer, Carl Henderson.

CARL. Hi.

NORA. But I'm—

PRUDENCE. *(Drags* NORA *to Right Center)* You will forgive us just barging in, won't you, darling?

NORA. I—

PRUDENCE. There. I knew you would. I just said so. *(Turning to* CARL*)* Didn't I just say so, Carl?

CARL. That's what she just said.

PRUDENCE. You see? *(She laughs lightly)* We just couldn't wait to see Grandma. Where is the great lady?

NORA. I'm afraid I don't know who—

PRUDENCE. Tatting. I'll bet—or sewing away on a sampler. Bless her great big, generous heart. You must tell me everything about her. Not just the important things but everything that makes our most famous grandmother tick.

NORA Grandmother who?

PRUDENCE. Listen, Carl. Grandmother who? *(She laughs)*

    (CARL *laughs. They* BOTH *look at* NORA *and she laughs in self-defense.*)

You're just modest.

NORA. If I don't sound repetitious, Grandmother who?

PRUDENCE. Why, your wonderful, famous Grandma Let—

STAN. *(He runs down the stairs talking as he comes)* Now, I'll be Hoskins and you— *(He sees* NORA *and the* OTHERS*)* Oh, hello, Nora. *(Calling back up the stairs)* Wait a minute, Maude.

NORA. Hello, Stanley.

(There is a pause while STANLEY *waits for* NORA *to introduce him and she waits for* STAN *to introduce her.* STANLEY *crosses down to* NORA's *Right.)*

NORA *and* STAN. Aren't you going to introduce me?
STAN. *(To* PRUDENCE *and* CARL*)* Whose friends are you?
PRUDENCE. *(To* NORA*)* You're not Mrs. Nichols?
NORA. I tried to tell you I wasn't, but this is Mr. Nichols.
PRUDENCE. *(Another conquest to make. She turns on* STANLEY*)* Mr. Nichols. Let me take your hand. *(She does so)* You're the grandson, kin to the famous. I'm Prudence Harper and this is Carl Henderson. *Life Magazine* sent us down to interview the Grandmother of the Year.
STAN. What? *Life Magazine.*
CARL. Best circulation of any magazine of its type.
PRUDENCE. I can't wait another moment, Mr. Nichols. Where is she? Where is Grandma—
STAN. *(Shouting her down so* NORA *won't hear)* Nora, why don't you go home? Chris will call you later.
NORA. What should I go home for? I don't understand.
CARL. Neither do I.
STAN. Just go home. *(Starts to push her out French windows)* It's a secret—about Saturday night.
NORA. The masquerade?
STAN. Yes, the masquerade. We'll explain later.
NORA. *(Now off stage with* STAN*)* You'd better.
PRUDENCE. *(Speaking just above a whisper)* This whole thing just doesn't jell.
CARL. *(As he sits on the sofa)* Agreed.
PRUDENCE. We may be on the verge of something interesting, darling.
STAN. *(Reenters and crosses to* PRUDENCE *at*

Center) Neighbor. Friendly, but prying, you know. Now, where were we?
PRUDENCE. *(Deadly)* Right here waiting to meet Grandma Letty.
STAN. Yes. She'd love to see you, I know, but she's resting at the moment.
PRUDENCE. *(Sceptically)* Oh.
STAN. Yes. *(Patting his chest)* Her heart, you know.
PRUDENCE. I didn't know.
STAN. Years now. She works so hard on her books. Really takes it out of a woman her age.
PRUDENCE. I can imagine. *(Now she tries a more feminine approach— She sidles up to* STAN *and fairly purrs at him)* But if we could see her for just one minute.

(STAN *sneezes.)*

CARL. Yeah, just to get a picture.
STAN. *(Sneezes again)* I'm sorry, but do you mind. *(He takes the rose* PRUDENCE *is wearing off of her suit and heads for the French windows.)*
PRUDENCE. Not at all.
STAN. I'm allergic to them. They make me—me—me SNEEZE! *(He sneezes as he throws the rose outside.)*
PRUDENCE. Human interest— Grandma, too!
STAN. No, just me. *(He takes out a handkerchief and blows his nose)* It's not hereditary, I guess.
CARL. My mother used to hiccup whenever she drank dandelion wine.
PRUDENCE. That's *entirely* different.
CARL. How about the pictures?
STAN. I'm afraid Grandma won't permit photographs of herself, not even on the jackets of her books. Maybe you've noticed.
PRUDENCE. The whole country has noticed. That's why we're here.
STAN. Grandma's such a shy and retiring soul. She doesn't even like to see our friends when they drop by.

She thinks people don't understand her—they make her nervous. Particularly now that the whole world is crying, "Where is Grandma Letty?"

MAUDE. *(Hearing her cue, she rushes downstairs)* Here I am!

STAN. *(Rushes over to the stairs and pushes her back up them)*

(CARL *tried vainly to get his camera out of the case and get a picture.)*

No, you're not!

PRUDENCE. *(Crosses to* CARL) Why didn't you get a shot?

CARL. How was I to know she was coming down?

STAN. *(Coming back downstairs)* Imagine trying to run downstairs like that in her condition.

PRUENCE. Looked spry enough to me.

STAN. I tell you what:

PRUDENCE. What?

STAN. You come back late this afternoon and she'll give you an exclusive interview. I guarantee it. How's that?

PRUDENCE. Exclusive, huh?

STAN. Yes—all yours.

CARL. What say, Pru?

PRUDENCE. It's a deal, darling. About four-thirty?

STAN. Fine. We'll see you then.

PRUDENCE. *(Crosses up to door)* Carl, we'll find a hotel and settle in the bar.

CARL. With beer or is it on the expense account?

PRUDENCE. With martinis!—it is!

CARL. Good. *(He goes out.)*

PRUDENCE. *(To* STAN) And Grandma better be here. There's something rotten in Denmark.

STAN. Oh, Shakespeare. *(He laughs.)*

PRUDENCE. And here's a direct quote from Prudence Harper. He who backs out always get caught in the end. *(She turns around and exits.)*

STAN. *(Closes the door, leans against it, and sighs audibly. Goes to French windows, draws the drapes*

over them, then crosses back to the front door and locks it. Then he calls upstairs) Chris.
CHRIS. *(Offstage)* Yes.
STAN. The coast is clear.
CHRIS. All right. Come on, Maude.

(They come down the stairs, CHRIS first.)

MAUDE. Look at me.

(This is the first time STAN has had a chance to spend time looking at MAUDE. She has on the wig, shawl, and the glasses. Although the skirt is too long for her, she looks passably like a grandmother.)

STAN. That's perfect.
CHRIS. *(Crosses to STAN at Left Center)* What was the trouble down here?
STAN. *Life Magazine*—that's what the trouble was.
CHRIS. *Life?*
MAUDE. *Life?* Not for me! *(She starts to run up the stairs.)*
STAN. *(Catches her)* Maude, come down here.
MAUDE. I don't want to tangle with no magazine people.
STAN. *(Bringing her down Center)* You'll miss your big chance. This performance will make Topsy look pale.
MAUDE. My Topsy couldn't look pale. She was with burnt cork.
STAN. We're wasting time. You need a rehearsal.
MAUDE. Maybe Mr. Hoskins does, too.
STAN. You sit down here. You're Grandma Letty and I'm Hoskins.
MAUDE. *(As she sits in chair down Right)* My wig don't fit.
STAN. It looks fine.
CHRIS. Who am I supposed to be?
STAN. You're the audience.

CHRIS. *(Sits on Right arm of sofa)* Then I'll sit here.

STAN. Now, Maude, just answer my questions as you think Grandma Letty would.

MAUDE. *(Crosses her legs and looks anything but the typical grandmother)* Shoot!

CHRIS. Ready? Curtain.

STAN. *(Paces upstage to the bookcase. Trying to sound as he imagines Hoskins would)* Tell me, Grandma, why did you start writing?

MAUDE. Well, son, I liked it. *(To* CHRIS*)* How's that?

CHRIS. Fine. Just fine. But try to look pleasant.

STAN. Yes. Be happy—smile.

MAUDE. I'll try. *(She forces a smile and looks at* STAN *and* CHRIS.*)*

CHRIS. That's better.

STAN. *(Crosses down Right)* When did you start writing, Grandma?

MAUDE. Er—three or four years ago.

STAN. *(Prompting her)* Four.

MAUDE. Four— I just remembered. *(Looks to* CHRIS *for approval.)*

(CHRIS *nods.)*

STAN. *(Crosses Right)* Who's your favorite author?

MAUDE. *(Thinks a moment and then comes up with the answer)* Buck Rogers!

STAN. *(Leans against the door jamb)* No. No. He isn't an author.

MAUDE. *(Unhappily)* Isn't he?

STAN. He's a character.

MAUDE. How should I know? Here I am doing a part with no script. Can't you write it down?

STAN. How do I know what questions they'll ask you?

MAUDE. I thought I was just supposed to take a plaque and say "thanks."

STAN. That was before *Life* entered the picture.
CHRIS. You're doing fine, Maude. Let's try some more.
MAUDE. Make them easier.
STAN. *(Crosses to Center)* What's your favorite book?
MAUDE. *(Quickly)* "Forever Amber."
STAN. *(Turns front)* Oh, Maude, you're a sweet old Grandmother. Say something like "Tom Sawyer" or "Peter Pan."
MAUDE. It's a lie, but O.K. *(Makes a sour face)* "Peter Pan." Better?
CHRIS. Smile. Look like you mean it.
MAUDE. *(Smiles)* "Peter Pan."
CHRIS. There—that's right.
STAN. *(Trying not to lose his control)* Tell us, Grandma, what are your hobbies?
MAUDE. I like to see movies, and bowl, and in my day I was a hot number on a back porch.
STAN. No! No! No!

(CHRIS *laughs.*)

MAUDE. Isn't that what you call human interest?
STAN. Now try to understand this. *(Crosses to her)* You cook and sew and write cute stories. That's all. No back-porching.
MAUDE. Ain't I supposed to be normal?
STAN. Yes, but don't talk about it.
MAUDE. *(Rises and takes off the wig)* I quit. This isn't like Topsy.

(The PHONE *rings.*)

STAN. You convince her, Chris. I'll get the phone.
CHRIS. *(Crosses to* MAUDE*)* Maude, listen to me. We're just upset. You can understand that, can't you?
MAUDE. I guess so, but I'm upset, too. You can understand that.

CHRIS. Of course. *(She puts the wig back on* MAUDE.*)*
STAN. *(Into phone)* Hello—who?—Mr. Hoskins! *(Looks to* CHRIS *in terror.)*
CHRIS. Hoskins!
MAUDE. Hoskins!
STAN. He's here. *(Into phone)* This is Stanley Nichols, Mr. Hoskins.—No, she's resting just now— You did? By plane?—
(Another look to CHRIS, *who crosses up to him.)* Yes, it is quicker. See you then. Good-bye.
CHRIS. Oh, Stanley, so soon.
STAN. Let's get to work. He came by plane and is taking a taxi from the airport.
CHRIS. Then he'll be here right away.
STAN. *(Crossing down Center)* Are you ready, Maude?
MAUDE. *(Crosses to* STAN) Suppose I don't know the answers?
STAN. Remember this: when in doubt—faint!
MAUDE. Faint?
STAN. Yes.
MAUDE. I don't feel well.
STAN. You look well—that's all that matters.
MAUDE. I don't care how I look— I feel awful.
STAN. Chris, we'd better look more presentable. I'll put on a suit and you get into something neater.
CHRIS. I feel insulted, but I'll do it. *(Crosses to stairs.)*
STAN. *(As he and* CHRIS *start up the stairs)* You sit there and get under control. We'll be down before Hoskins gets here.
MAUDE. *(Sits in chair up Right)* O.K., but I don't guarantee nothing.
(STANLEY *and* CHRIS *exit upstairs.*)
(She sits still for a moment. A nervous look creeps over her face. She begins muttering to herself) "Tom Sawyer." "Peter Pan." No, Maude, look pleasant. *(Smiles)* "Peter Pan." *(She realizes it's no good and*

tries again with a laugh) "Peter Pan." *(The PHONE rings and she jumps. Calls upstairs)* I'll answer it. *(Picks up phone and talks into it)* Hello—oh, you must want— Grandma Letty? Why, that's me. *(She looks up the stairs hopelessly, looking for help)* United Newsreel! But I—me in the movies? Oh, dear— What do I have to say?—Well, I— I like "Peter Pan." *(She laughs)* —This afternoon? No! No movies. I'm busy writing "Grandma Letty Meets Tom Sawyer." Goodbye. *(She hangs up)* Movies! *(She mops her brow with the shawl and pushes the wig back on her head.)*

CHRIS. *(Upstairs)* Who was it, Maude?

MAUDE. Oh—wrong number.

CHRIS. We'll be down in a minute.

MAUDE. *(To herself)* Wrong number—that's me! *(Slumps in the footstool and puts her elbows on her knees)* I've got to think. Hoskins. Life Magazine. Newsreel photographers. Maude, this ain't your cup of tea. No, sir. *(Takes off the wig and remainder of the costume as she talks)* Just go quietly, that's what you've got to do. Leave them to stew in their own stew. You just ain't right for this part. *(She crosses to the phone table and writes a note on the pad. Rips off the paper and leaves it on the pile of clothes on the stool)* There.

(She goes to the front door, but when she is almost there, the door knob turns and someone outside rattles it.)

It's him!

(The DOORBELL rings.)

(MAUDE looks around for a quick escape, sees the French windows and darts out them.)

(The DOORBELL rings again.)

CHRIS. *(Upstairs)* Stan, it's the front door.

STAN. *(Upstairs)* It couldn't be Hoskins so soon.

CHRIS. *(Upstairs)* Maude, don't answer it. Wait for us. Hurry, Stan.

STAN. *(Upstairs)* I am.

(From outside the French windows come the voices of BRADLEY *and* PEGGY.*)*

PEGGY. *(Offstage)* This is open.
BRAD. *(Offstage)* Why was the front door locked?
PEGGY. *(She enters and crosses above the sofa followed by* BRADLEY*)* How should I know?
BRAD. Maybe they're all out.
PEGGY. Maude must be here. *(Crosses to the foot of the stairs. Calling)* Anyone home?
CHRIS. *(Upstairs)* Hi, Peggy.
PEGGY. Why was the front door locked?
CHRIS. *(Upstairs)* The door? Oh, I told Maude not to answer it.
PEGGY. Where is she?
CHRIS. *(Upstairs)* Isn't she there?
PEGGY. No.
STAN. *(Upstairs)* She isn't!
PEGGY. Is anything wrong?

*(*STAN *runs down the stairs pulling his coat on.)*

BRAD. What's going on?
STAN. Bradley, you'd better go. *(Runs to the kitchen door.)*
BRAD. *(Surprised)* Go?
PEGGY. Stan, what's the matter with you?
STAN. *(Calling out kitchen door)* Maude! Maude!
PEGGY. *(Crosses Center)* What is it?
STAN. *(Turns to* PEGGY*)* Hoskins is due here any minute.
PEGGY. No!
BRAD. Cyril B. Hoskins, the publisher?
PEGGY. Yes. Stan, what are you going to do?
STAN. Find Maude. *(Exits calling)* Maude!
BRAD. *(Sits calmly on the sofa)* I'd love to meet a real publisher.

PEGGY. Stan's right—you'd better go.
BRAD. Why can't I stay and meet him?
STAN. *(Enters on the run and sees the costume)* Look!
PEGGY. *(Pulls BRADLEY to his feet)* Because he and Stan want to talk private business.
STAN. *(Sees the note on the costume and starts to read it)* Very private!
BRAD. About the new book?
PEGGY. Yes, the book.
BRAD. *(As PEGGY starts pushing him through the French windows)* Can I meet him later?

(PEGGY, *in response, sneezes.*)

STAN. *(Having read the note)* No! No! No!
PEGGY. *(As she successfully gets BRADLEY out of the room)* Good-bye, Brad. Come over later.
STAN. *(Runs to the foot of the stairs and calls)* Chris, Chris, come here. Emergency!
BRAD. *(Off stage)* I hope you'll be in a more receptive mood.

(PEGGY *comes in, closes the French windows and locks them.*)

CHRIS. *(Runs down the stairs)* What's the matter?
STAN. Listen to this. *(Reading MAUDE's note)* "Topsy rehearsed longer than Grandma. Gone to movie. Good luck. Maude."
PEGGY. *(Crosses in to CHRIS)* What's that mean?
CHRIS. Maude was going to impersonate Grandma Letty for Hoskins.
STAN. And the press! *(Gives up and sits in the chair up Right)* Well, that's the end of our bread and butter.
CHRIS. Stan, you'll just have to tell the truth.
STAN. There must be a way out. *(Sees the wig in front of him and gets an idea)* Chris, you can be

Grandma Letty. *(Picks up the wig and heads for* Chris.)
    Chris. Me?
    Stan. Why not?
    Chris. I'm no actress— I'd laugh.
    Stan. *(Puts the wig on her)* Look, it fits.
    Chris. *(Takes off the wig)* Don't be silly. I'd never get away with it.
    Stan. *(Takes the wig from* Chris) Someone's got to— Peggy! *(He rushes towards her, wig in hand.)*
    Peggy. *(Backing away from him to corner of the hallway)* Hey, leave me alone.
    Stan. *(Puts the wig on her. It is slightly askew and makes a grotesque sight)* That'll never do.
    Peggy. You bet it won't. *(Gives him the wig.)*

(DOORBELL rings.)

    Stan. That's him! Hoskins!
    Peggy. The door's still locked.
    Stan. What'll we do?
    Peggy. I don't know.
    Chris. Oh, Stanley—tell him.

(DOORBELL rings again.)

    Hoskins. *(From outside the door—in a jovial voice)* Hello, in there.
    Peggy. Pretend we're out.
    Stan. He'd only come back.
    Hoskins. Hello, open the door.
    Stan. *(Shakes the wig at the door)* Shut up!
    Hoskins. *(Getting angry)* What? Who's in there?

(DOORBELL rings again insistently.)

    Stan. We'll have to answer it!
    Peggy. *(Heads for the French windows)* I'm leaving.

CHRIS. Don't go—this is a family crisis.
STAN. But someone's got to— *(Looks at the wig)* I've got it. I've got it! *(Puts on the wig.)*
CHRIS. Stanley, no!
PEGGY. You're crazy.
HOSKINS. *(Furious)* Open this door! Where's Grandma Letty?

(DOORBELL rings again, then HOSKINS starts pounding on the door furiously.)

STAN. Give me those clothes— I'll get away with it. *(He grabs the costume and runs back to the foot of the stairs.)*
PEGGY. You can't do it—what will people say?
STAN. *(As he runs up the stairs)* The hell with what people say—this is money!
CHRIS. *(Rushing to the foot of the stairs)* Oh, Stanley!
PEGGY. *(Crossing upstage to CHRIS)* Shall we open it?

(The POUNDING and DOORBELL continue at intervals.)

HOSKINS. Open up or I'll break it down!
CHRIS. It looks like we'll have to. Ready?
PEGGY. I guess so.
CHRIS *(Seeing the bottle on the table downstage Right)* The whiskey—hide it.
PEGGY. O.K. *(Puts it behind books in bookcase.)*
CHRIS. Smile.

(They force a smile. CHRIS unlocks the door.)

HOSKINS. For the last time—

(CHRIS opens the door and HOSKINS, pounding violently at it, falls into the room. He is, by now, dis-

heveled. *The plaque, wrapped in plain brown paper, falls to the floor beside him.)*

CHRIS. *(Smiling. The polite hostess)* Do come in.

(As HOSKINS looks up at PEGGY and CHRIS, there is a loud CRASH from upstairs as if someone had fallen over a chair. Someone did. It was STAN. He screams "Oh, hell." The three people in the living room look up the stairs as

THE CURTAIN FALLS

ACT TWO

STAN *is again heard yelling "Oh, hell," then the Curtain opens showing* CHRIS, PEGGY, *and* HOSKINS *in the same positions as they were at the end of Act One. There is no time lapse.* CYRIL B. HOSKINS *is an elderly man with tremendous vitality. His prime interest in life is book sales and Hoskins & Company, publishers. At times, he is sentimental, but never loses sight of business for an instant. He has a full head of white hair, wears a busines suit, and carries the inevitable pill box in his vest coat pocket.*

HOSKINS. *(Still on his knees)* What was that?
CHRIS. What, Mr. Hoskins?
HOSKINS. That swearing.
CHRIS. Oh, that. Why—it's the plumber. *(To* PEGGY*)* Isn't it, Peggy?
PEGGY. Yes, the plumber.
CHRIS. He's having a hard time.
PEGGY. Won't you come in?
CHRIS. There's no use sitting there in the doorway.
HOSKINS. *(As* CHRIS *helps him to his feet)* Thank you.

(CHRIS *closes the door as* HOSKINS *comes into the room with the plaque.)*

CHRIS. I'm Mrs. Nichols and this is my niece, Peggy.
PEGGY. How do you do?
HOSKINS. *(Brushes himself off)* I am Cyril B. Hoskins of Hoskins & Co., publishers, and I want to know what's going on here.

CHRIS. *(Crosses to his Right)* Nothing—nothing at all, Mr. Hoskins.
PEGGY. *(At* HOSKINS' *Left)* Not a thing.
HOSKINS. I fly all the way out to this Godforsaken territory, get yelled at by some plumber, and refused entry to see Grandma Letty.
CHRIS. Refused entry, but Mr. Hoskins—
HOSKINS. But nothing! Where is she? Is she all right?
CHRIS. Of course, but—
HOSKINS. Will you stop butting at me and tell me what you've done with her?
CHRIS. *(Losing her patience)* We've done nothing with her. We just didn't hear the doorbell, that's all.
HOSKINS. Didn't hear it? Someone yelled at me to shut up.
CHRIS. I'll have my husband speak to that plumber.
HOSKINS. Your husband—would that be Stanley Nichols?
CHRIS. It would.
HOSKINS. That crack-pot!
CHRIS. Mr. Hoskins!
HOSKINS. *(His hand to his stomach)* Don't let me get upset— I must rest—sit down.
  (CHRIS *sits* HOSKINS *on the sofa.)*
May I have a glass of water?
CHRIS. Peggy?
PEGGY. O.K. *(Exits into the kitchen.)*
HOSKINS. *(Takes out a small pill-box from his vest pocket)* My stomach, Mrs. Nichols—nervous disorder. Strain of running the largest publishing house in the country.
CHRIS. Well, you just relax right there. Let me take that. *(She starts to take the plaque.)*
HOSKINS. No. *(He holds onto it with both hands)* This is for Grandma Letty and no one else.
PEGGY. *(Reenters with glass of water)* Here you are, Mr. Hoskins.

(CHRIS *crosses above sofa.*)

HOSKINS. Thank you.
(CHRIS *and* PEGGY *exchange frantic looks as* HOSKINS *takes a pill.*)
Ah! I feel better now. (*Puts the glass on the coffee table.*)

CHRIS. That's good.

HOSKINS. Now for the long-anticipated moment—Where is Grandma Letty?

PEGGY. Upstairs.

CHRIS. She's changing. She just got up from her nap.

HOSKINS. (*Smiles*) How typical of Grandma to take an afternoon nap.

CHRIS. Yes, typical.

HOSKINS. Dear Grandma.

CHRIS. Dear Grandma.

PEGGY. (*Looks to* CHRIS) Ah, yes, dear Grandma!

CHRIS. (*Breaks the serene moment*) Mr. Hoskins, why did you call my husband a crack-pot?

HOSKINS. Because he is one. That first draft of his book he sent me—

PEGGY. You mean the long, tragic one?

HOSKINS. Has he written any other?

CHRIS. Oh, yes,—one or two.

PEGGY. But not like that.

HOSKINS. It was undoubtedly the worst, most amateurish thing I have ever read.

CHRIS. Oh, no.

HOSKINS. Oh, yes.

CHRIS. Poor Stan.

HOSKINS. Didn't you know about it?

CHRIS. I knew he was working on a book, of course, but I had no idea he'd mailed you a draft.

(PEGGY *sits chair down Right.*)

HOSKINS. The nerve. The sheer, unbrazen nerve.

CHRIS. *(Crosses to the sofa and sits)* But, Mr. Hoskins, shouldn't writers submit their material? What else are publishers for?

HOSKINS. They should submit it, yes. That's how we find and develop our authors. But your husband had Grandma Letty submit it for him—thinking he could squeeze by on her reputation.

PEGGY. And you didn't like it?

HOSKINS. An understatement. Mr. Nichols evidently wanted to point up a philosophy of his own, that people should learn to think for themselves. I don't happen to agree. If the American people could think for themselves, our comic book department would have to shut down. Where would Spaceman be? And Bat-Boy?

CHRIS. I see your point.

HOSKINS. It's all well and good to philosophize, but an author shouldn't beat his readers over their collective heads.

PEGGY. What you mean is that Uncle Stanley isn't as talented an author as Grandma Letty?

HOSKINS. *(Throws his head back and laughs)* My dear, they are like night and day.

PEGGY. Really?

(PEGGY *and* CHRIS *exchange a look.*)

HOSKINS. But where is she? I have waited so many years— I can't hold back another moment.

CHRIS. I'll call and see. *(Crosses to foot of stairs and calls)* Grandma!

STAN. *(His voice comes from upstairs. It is now that of "Grandma Letty," or rather* STAN's *idea of Grandma Letty. It is old and cracked and yet pleasant. And it is unique)* Yes, dear.

HOSKINS. *(Rises)* Her voice.

PEGGY. *(Looks at* CHRIS) That's what it was.

CHRIS. *(Calling)* Mr. Hoskins is here.

STAN. *(Upstairs)* Tell the dear man to wait. I'll be right down.

CHRIS. *(Turning to* HOSKINS *and crossing back into the room)* Just one minute, Mr. Hoskins.

HOSKINS. *(Crosses to* CHRIS) I heard. To think, I am about to meet the idol of millions. I should bow in homage.

CHRIS. *(At a loss what else to say)* Would you like a drink while we're waiting?

HOSKINS. *(Horrified)* Drink? Of what?

CHRIS. Scotch, rye, bourbon, and I think we have a little gin.

HOSKINS. Scotch. Gin. Alcoholic beverages in the same house with Grandma Letty, I can't believe it.

PEGGY. Neither can I. I didn't know we had any liquor.

CHRIS. *(Realizes her mistake)* As a matter of fact, we keep it hidden.

HOSKINS. Hidden?

CHRIS. Yes, in—in the washing machine. *(Looks to* PEGGY *for help.)*

PEGGY. We only serve it to company.

HOSKINS. I see.

CHRIS. *(Crosses down to* PEGGY) Once Grandma did some laundry and it came out bourbon bleached.

(CHRIS *and* PEGGY *laugh weakly.*)

HOSKINS. *(Crosses to French windows)* Grandma only drinks herb tea.

CHRIS. Why, Mr. Hoskins, however did you guess?

HOSKINS I know all about the great lady

PEGGY. You do?

HOSKINS. *(Crosses in to Left of sofa)* From her books. From her wonderful books. It's four years now since I read the first one. What a moment that was—like reading the first draft of the Magna Charta. The script had passed through all of the company readers and finally came to rest on my desk. It sat there like a beacon light in the darkness of my life.

CHRIS. That's beautiful, Mr. Hoskins.

HOSKINS. I could have been a writer, too, you know.
CHRIS. I bet you could.
HOSKINS. I picked it up and started to read. From the first paragraph, I knew it was great. By the time I finished "Grandma Letty and the Hen Who Wouldn't Lay an Egg," I was a different person, a changed man. *(He takes out his handkerchief)* Tears were in my eyes, Mrs. Nichols. Suddenly I realized the futility of my life, the time I had wasted in merely amassing a fortune. There's a deeper adult meaning in all of Grandma's books. I'll wager as many adults read them as do children. *(He blows his nose.)*
PEGGY. *(Not quite believing what she hears)* And just from reading her stories, you feel you know her?
HOSKINS. Perfectly. *(Crosses to the Center)* From the first, I respected her desire for no personal publicity, but now she has snowballed into such a national figure, we must introduce her to the public. She's taken the place of Lana Turner and Joe DiMaggio in the hearts of millions, requests are pouring in for her pin-up pictures. I doubt if Grandma Moses will ever paint again.
CHRIS. I do hope you won't be disappointed in her.
HOSKINS. Disappointed? Was Anthony disappointed in Cleopatra? Napoleon in Josephine? Abercrombie in Fitch? No, I shall not be disappointed. Grandma will be—just Grandma.
PEGGY. I certainly hope so.
HOSKINS. *(Crosses down Left)* I can see her in everything about this room.
CHRIS. *(Sits on the arm of the down Right Chair)* You can?
HOSKINS. I see her sitting there *(Pointing to sofa)* stitching away on a sampler, her grey hair gently curling around her cherubic face, a shawl drawn over her little body.
PEGGY. She's not exactly little.
HOSKINS. No?
CHRIS. No. She's almost six feet.

HOSKINS. Six feet!!
PEGGY. Funniest thing—she comes from a long line of Amazon-like women.

(HOSKINS *looks at* CHRIS.)

CHRIS. Not from my side—from Stanley's family tree.
PEGGY. Remember Aunt Edith? Six feet three in her stocking feet.
HOSKINS. Amazing. But what difference does height make? *(He pounds his chest)* It's what's in here, in her heart that counts.
PEGGY. You were right about the grey hair though.
CHRIS. And there's another unusual thing.
PEGGY. *(Bewildered)* Yes, another.
HOSKINS. *(To* PEGGY*)* What's that?
PEGGY. *(Not knowing, turns to* CHRIS*)* Tell him, Chris.
CHRIS. Her complexion, Mr. Hoskins.
PEGGY. *(Catching on)* Of course—her complexion.
CHRIS. So young looking—it's really unbelievable.
PEGGY. Everyone remarks on it. She's the envy of the neighborhood.

(STAN *comes down the stairs. He is dressed as Grandma Letty. He wears the same skirt, wig, shawl, and glasses that* CHRIS *first wore. In addition, he has on a blouse which is long, full-sleeved and high at the neck. On his feet are men's carpet slippers. He is very nervous and during the following speech tip-toes down the stairs.)*

HOSKINS. Grandma Letty is the envy of all women. She has the grace, the beauty, the elegance that time cannot erase. Four years of waiting is at an end. I know now how Stanley felt when he said, "Mr. Livingston, I presume." I must see her.

STAN. *(In Grandma's sweet voice)* Then turn around.
HOSKINS. *(As they ALL rise)* Grandma!
STAN. Mr. Hoskins, I presume.
HOSKINS. *(Crosses to STAN, who extends a hand. HOSKINS kneels and kisses it)* This is the greatest moment of my life.
STAN. Rise, Mr. Hoskins.
HOSKINS. *(Rising)* To think that I—that you— I can't believe it.
STAN. Do let us sit down while you recover.
HOSKINS. *(As he helps STAN to the sofa)* Let me help you, my dear.
STAN. I see that chivalry is not dead.
HOSKINS. Chivalry only dies when it has no inspiration.
STAN. *(Sits on Right end of sofa and smiles sweetly at HOSKINS who sits on Left end of sofa)* How sweet! Thank you.
HOSKINS. You're more than welcome.
STAN. *(Tolerantly to CHRIS)* You can sit down, too, Chris.

(CHRIS *sits in chair up Right and* PEGGY *sits in chair down Right.*)

CHRIS. *(Glaring at him)* Thank you.
STAN. You're more than welcome.
CHRIS. *(Mischievously)* I was just wondering if you wanted me to go up and get your knitting?
STAN. Knitting?
CHRIS. Yes, your knitting.
STAN. *(Turning front)* No, dear—definitely no.
CHRIS. Mr. Hoskins won't mind, will you?
HOSKINS. I would consider it an honor to see our foremost authoress being domestic.
CHRIS. Peggy, will you get it, please? It's on my dresser.
STAN. No, dear. I want to give my undivided attention to Mr. Hoskins.

ACT II MORE THAN MEETS THE EYE 55

PEGGY. *(As she starts for the stairs)* I don't mind, Grandma. I love to watch you knit.
STAN. *(Thinking fast)* It's not there. I— I lost it.
CHRIS. What a shame—where?
STAN. Where? Oh,—on the picnic last weekend.
CHRIS. Well, I found it in the car. Go on, Peggy.

(PEGGY *runs upstairs.*)

STAN. But I don't—
HOSKINS. *(Pats* STAN'S *hand, which* STAN *quickly withdraws)* Now, now, Grandma. Don't let me disturb you. Go right ahead with your usual routine—knit, bake your pie, whatever you want.
STAN. I'm just taking life easy. I haven't been well lately.
HOSKINS. Nothing serious, I hope.
STAN. My heart. I have to cut down on my activities.
HOSKINS. *(Afraid for his income)* Not your writing?
STAN. Not that. Don't worry, Mr. Hoskins, I'm full of ideas.
CHRIS. You'd be surprised what ideas.

(STAN *glares at* CHRIS.)

STAN. *(Turning to* HOSKINS. *Anxious to get the ordeal over with)* And now the plaque.
HOSKINS. *(Laughs)* Not yet, dear lady. After all these years, do you think I'm going to rush away?
STAN. But I can't wait a—
HOSKINS. Besides there are some others coming. They forced your address out of me.
STAN. What others?
HOSKINS. Newsreel photographers, the Associated Press, and *Life Magazine.*
STAN. I saw the magazine people already.
HOSKINS. You did?

STAN. *(Realizes his slip)* I mean my grandson, Stanley, did. He told me about it.

CHRIS. They tell each other everything.

HOSKINS. Where is this grandson?

STAN. He's upstairs working.

HOSKINS. I was just telling Mrs. Nichols about him. If I may speak candidly, I suggest you don't let him handle your affairs any longer. What you need is a good business manager, Grandma.

STAN. Stanley does just fine. Being a writer himself, he understands my problems.

HOSKINS. Grandma, you may not believe this, but he actually sent me one of his manuscripts with your name endorsing it.

STAN. *(Trying to change the subject so* CHRIS *won't find out)* Let's not talk business now.

CHRIS. It's all right, Grandma. Mr. Hoskins told me all about it.

STAN. *(Weakly)* All?

CHRIS. *(Deadly)* All!

STAN. Did he? *(Slaps* HOSKINS *affectionately)* Why, the old scamp!

CHRIS. And do you know what Mr. Hoskins' opinion of the book is?

STAN. *(Turns to* HOSKINS) No. What?

HOSKINS. Unadulterated drivel.

STAN. Stanley's book?

HOSKINS. Most disappointing. Are you sure you read it?

STAN. Of course I read it. I thought it was great—a magnificient work.

HOSKINS. Let's not spoil our first meeting with arguing over an inferior author.

(PEGGY *comes downstairs with* CHRIS' *knitting.*)

STAN. *(Anxious to change the subject)* Let's have a drink.

PEGGY. *(Pointedly to* STAN*)* It's in the washing machine.
STAN. What is?
PEGGY. Something you shouldn't know about.
HOSKINS. *(Incredulously)* You want a drink, Grandma?
STAN. *(Thinking fast)* Orange crush—oh, yes, dear old orange crush.
PEGGY. Of course. I'll get it. *(Gives knitting to* STAN*)* Here, Grandma, your knitting.
STAN. *(Dryly)* Thanks.

(PEGGY *goes into the kitchen.*)

HOSKINS. What are you making, Grandma?
STAN. *(Holds up knitting and tries to decide)* Why, it's a—a—an—a sweater! That's what it is—a sweater.
HOSKINS. *(Smiles)* A sweater. How wonderful.
STAN. Yes, for Christine. *(Smiles sweetly at* CHRIS.*)*
HOSKINS. How thoughtful.
STAN. I can't wait to finish it.
CHRIS. I can't wait to wear it.
HOSKINS. Go on, Grandma, I'd love to watch you knit.
CHRIS. So would I.

(CHRIS *and* HOSKINS *lean forward.*)

STAN. *(Determined to show them)* All right. *(Defiantly takes hold of the knitting, tries to decide the top from the bottom, the beginning from the end. Finally, he plunges ahead and jabs with the loose needle. The whole thing falls onto the floor)* Oops-a-daisy!
HOSKINS. *(Rushes to pick it up)* Let me.

(While HOSKINS *is bent over,* STAN *makes a menacing gesture at* CHRIS.*)*

STAN. *(As* HOSKINS *give him the knitting)* Thank you.

(Hoskins *sits on the sofa again.*)
Well, now. (*He plows into it again, works his way through a few stitches, realizes* EVERYONE *is looking at him, and speaks*) Go right on talking. Don't let me interrupt.

HOSKINS. Oh, yes. (*Turns to* CHRIS) Tell me how it feels, Mrs. Nichols, to be living in the same house with a famous author.

CHRIS. It feels just wonderful, Mr. Hoskins. (*She stares at* STAN.)

(HOSKINS *turns and stares, too.* STAN'S *tongue is sticking out and moving as the knitting needles move from side to side. Finally he looks up to find the other two staring at him. He drops a stitch.*)

STAN. I've been thinking, Christine, this pattern isn't any good for you, so— (*He pulls out the needles and starts rolling the wool back onto the ball.*)

CHRIS. (*Horrified*) No! No! Don't!

STAN. (*As he puts the mess of knitting on the coffee table*) There. Now I feel better.

PEGGY. (*Enters with four glasses of orange crush on a tray*) Here we are. (*Crosses above the sofa and offers one to* HOSKINS) Mr. Hoskins?

HOSKINS. (*Obviously wishing it were anything but what it is*) Thank you. If it's good enough for Grandma Letty, it's good enough for me.

PEGGY. (*Having given one to* STAN, *crosses and offers one to* CHRIS) Chris?

CHRIS. No, thanks.

STAN. (*Glaring at* CHRIS) Go on, dear, drink it.

CHRIS. (*Definitely*) No, thank you.

STAN. (*Offering a toast after* PEGGY *has put the tray on the table down Right and sat*) Here's to the four of us.

HOSKINS *and* PEGGY. The four of us.

(*They drink and* HOSKINS *chokes violently.*)

HOSKINS. Water! Water! *(Continues choking.)*
PEGGY. I'll get it. *(She runs into the kitchen.)*
CHRIS. *(Slaps* HOSKINS *on the back)* Take a deep breath.
HOSKINS. *(Husky-voice, trying to speak)* I—I can't!
STAN. *(Rises and goes to* HOSKINS *above sofa. He pushes* CHRIS *aside)* Let me. *(He puts* HOSKINS' *arms above his head and slaps him violently on the back.)*
HOSKINS. All right. All right. Went down the wrong way, that's all.
STAN. *(Smiling happily)* Feeling better?
PEGGY. *(Enters from the kitchen with the glass of water)* Here.
HOSKINS. *(Taking the water and a pill from his pillbox)* Thank you.
STAN. Pills, Mr. Hoskins?
HOSKINS. Yes—stomach trouble.
STAN. *(Happily)* And me with my heart. Birds of a feather. *(He laughs as merrily as is possible for him)* Now, why don't you give me the plaque and we'll have the hallowed moment alone—just the four of us?
HOSKINS. I should wait for the others.
STAN. I don't like people in lumps, Mr. Hoskins—just one at a time. Why not give me the plaque now? *(He reaches out his hands.)*
HOSKINS. *(Picking up the plaque)* All right, if that's the way you want it. *(Starts to unwrap it)* I am presenting this in behalf of Lawton Ellerbe, president of the Foundation for Better Futures for Grandmothers, and I—
(The front DOORBELL rings.)
That must be the people from *Life Magazine*.
STAN. They weren't supposed to come back until four-thirty. At least that's what Stanley said.
PEGGY. They probably have a nose for news.

(DOORBELL rings.)

CHRIS. Someone's got to answer it. *(As she crosses up to the door)* Our maid's at a matinee.

HOSKINS. Matinee?

STAN. *(Anxious not to be seen by anyone else)* I'd better go upstairs and freshen up.

HOSKINS. You look fine as you are.

STAN. Just a few moments, dear Mr. Hoskins—we women, you know.

HOSKINS. *(Kissing STAN's hand)* Till then.

STAN. Till then. *(He pats HOSKINS' face and hurries up the stairs waving the fringe of his shawl after him.)*

PEGGY. *(As she follows STAN)* I'll help you. Excuse me, Mr. Hoskins.

HOSKINS. *(Crosses down Left)* Of course, my dear.

(CHRIS *opens the front door.* PRUDENCE *and* CARL *stand there.*)

PRUDENCE. *(Using her usual approach)* You must be Mrs. Nichols. I'm Prudence Harper and this is Carl Henderson.

CARL. Hi.

PRUDENCE. We're from *Life Magazine*.

CHRIS. Yes, my husband told me. Won't you come in?

PRUDENCE. Thanks, darling.

(She enters the room followed by CARL. CHRIS *closes the door.)*

(PRUDENCE *sees* HOSKINS *and her smile fades)* Well, Hoskie, I thought you weren't due until later.

HOSKINS. *(Curtly)* I took a plane.

PRUDENCE. Trying to pull a fast one? I've been promised an exclusive, darling. It that clear?

HOSKINS. Don't worry, Pru.

PEGGY. *(Calling from upstairs)* Chris.

CHRIS. Yes.

PEGGY. *(Upstairs)* Grandma wants you a minute.

CHRIS. I bet she does. Excuse me. *(She exits upstairs.)*

PRUDENCE. Well, Hoskie, where are you hiding this children's answer to Dorothy Dix?

ACT II MORE THAN MEETS THE EYE   61

HOSKINS. Grandma's freshening up.
PRUDENCE. *(Always prying, she notices the knitting and picks it up)* Who's she think she is anyway—Winston Churchill never kept me waiting.
HOSKINS. Now, Pru, Grandma's a great and wonderful lady. She's on the road to becoming one of the most important women alive today.
CARL. *(Gets his camera ready)* How about some pics? You know—family background, sweet, old homestead?
PRUDENCE. You mean like the zoo—seen in her natural habitat?
CARL. Yeah— I guess so.
PRUDENCE. O.K. then, take one of the great lady's living room.
CARL. It'll lack interest.
PRUDENCE. Maybe you can sell it to *House Beautiful*.
CARL. *(Sits on the stool to adjust camera)* You're the boss.
HOSKINS. She doesn't want any photographs taken.
PRUDENCE. The shy type, huh?
HOSKINS. Shy and retiring.
PRUDENCE. Listen, darling, no one shies from publicity. It makes money and we all like that, don't we, Hoskie?
CARL. *(Snaps a picture from down Right)* Got it—what now?
PRUDENCE. Better wait until the divine lady gets herself down here.
HOSKINS. She won't let you take any.
PRUDENCE. *(To* CARL*)* Then try and sneak one. Are you sure you don't need flash?
CARL. *(Patting his camera)* Not with this baby. *(Puts camera on footstool and crosses to the bookcase)* I sneaked that shot of Ike and Mamie through the fire escape window without flash, didn't I?
HOSKINS. I don't think you should take any pictures

without Grandma's permission. It might upset her when she finds out and she has a weak heart.

PRUDENCE. We don't have to worry if she can stomach her own books.

CARL. *(Agreeing readily)* Yeah.

PRUDENCE. Thanks for the confirmation, darling. *(To* HOSKINS*)* You want book sales to rise, don't you, Hoskie?

HOSKINS. *(Sits sofa Left)* Well, you know how it is.

PRUDENCE. I'm glad we understand each other. *(Crosses away up Center as she thinks)* Now if we could only get something sensational like Grandma smoking opium.

HOSKINS. Never. There's nothing about Grandma that isn't kind and gentle and good.

PRUDENCE. You have your ideas and I have mine.

MAUDE. *(Enters through the front door and sees the unexpected people)* Oh, excuse me.

HOSKINS. Come right in.

PRUDENCE. Yes, do.

MAUDE. *(Enters uncertainly)* Thanks.

PRUDENCE. Can we help you?

MAUDE. I'm the maid.

CARL. Bartender, too?

MAUDE. Huh?

CARL. Skip it.

PRUDENCE. Carl!

HOSKINS. Did you enjoy the matinee?

MAUDE. You mean the movie?

HOSKINS. Yes.

MAUDE. I didn't go.

PRUDENCE. *(Crosses down Center)* We're just waiting for Grandma Letty.

MAUDE. I imagine you are. I'll just put my things in the kitchen and she'll be right with you.

PRUDENCE. It's about time.

MAUDE. She would have been here sooner, but I did something kind of mean.

PRUDENCE. What's that?

MAUDE. I just didn't do a duty I should have done, but things will be all right now. I got my courage back again. *(She exits into the kitchen.)*

PRUDENCE. *(After a pause. Looking after MAUDE)* That was one of the most confused conversations in which I have ever participated.

HOSKINS. Didn't understand it myself.

PRUDENCE. *(To CARL who has been looking through the books in the bookcase)* Carl, you're not going to read?

CARL. Don't be stupid.

HOSKINS. Then what are you looking for?

CARL. *(Removes book and there is a bottle of whiskey which PEGGY put there earlier)* Found it!

PRUDENCE. One gold medal for you.

CARL. People always hide liquor behind books.

PRUDENCE. "Grandma Drinks"—what a headline.

HOSKINS. It must be orange crush.

CARL. *(Taking a swallow)* If it is, it's ninety proof!

(PRUDENCE *takes the bottle.*)

HOSKINS. It's that grandson of hers. Pru, don't mention him in the interview.

PRUDENCE. I thought he was kind of cute.

HOSKINS. Cute? He's a leech on Grandma's bank account. The wife is sweet though.

CHRIS. *(Upstairs. Calling back to STAN)* Hurry up, Stan. We'll be downstairs.

PRUDENCE. Here they come. *(Gives the bottle to CARL who puts it on the bottom shelf.)*

CHRIS. *(As she comes downstairs with PEGGY)* Sorry to keep you waiting.

PRUDENCE. That's perfectly all right.

CHRIS. Miss Harper, I'd like you to meet my niece, Peggy. *(To PEGGY)* This is Miss Harper and Mr. Henderson.

PEGGY. How do you do?

HOSKINS. Where's Grandma? We're ready for the presentation now.

CHRIS. She'll be right down. Wouldn't you all like a drink—

PEGGY. *(Finishing the sentence)* Of orange crush?

PRUDENCE. No whiskey in the house, I suppose?

CHRIS. Of course not.

CARL. Oh, there isn't. *(Holds up the bottle.)*

CHRIS. Oh, that. *(She turns to PEGGY and she laughs.)*

PRUDENCE. Should make an interesting footnote to the interview.

CHRIS. *(Confidentially)* It's our maid—drinks like a fish. She's always hiding the stuff.

STAN. *(Comes down the stairs in the suit he was wearing at the end of Act One)* Miss Harper, Mr. Henderson, I'm so glad you came back. *(Crosses to HOSKINS)* And this must be Mr. Hoskins. I'm Stanley Nichols.

HOSKINS. *(Coldly)* Oh, yes.

STAN. *(Grabbing HOSKINS' unoffered hand)* So nice to meet you.

    (PEGGY *and* CHRIS *retire up Left and* STAN *crosses to* PRUDENCE.)

I do wish you could have seen Grandma.

PRUDENCE. We're waiting, darling.

STAN. Unfortunately, she's taken to her bed.

HOSKINS. But why? She was fine ten minutes ago.

STAN. The excitement was too much for her. So, if you'll let me stand in for Grandma, do the interview, and take the plaque, all will be well.

CARL. No pictures?

STAN. I'm afraid not.

PRUDENCE. *(Getting angry)* Just a minute.

BRAD. *(Appears at the French windows and tries to get PEGGY's attention)* Pssst.

PEGGY. *(As everyone turns to look)* Bradley.

(MAUDE *sneaks in from the kitchen and goes up the*

stairs while EVERYONE *is turned to the French windows and* BRADLEY.)

BRAD. Peggy, I have to see you—about what happened earlier today.
PEGGY. But I can't leave now.
BRAD. You'll have to or it's the end.
PEGGY. It can't be the end—it hasn't begun yet.
CHRIS. *(Crossing to them)* Run along, you two. Take a walk around the garden.
PEGGY. Are you sure you can manage without me?
CHRIS. Who knows? But go on anyway.
PEGGY. *(To the* OTHERS *in the room while she exits)* Excuse me. Come on, Brad.
BRAD. Now don't start sneezing.
PEGGY. I may have to.

(They are out.)

CHRIS. Adolescent troubles. You remember how it was.
PRUDENCE. I remember—it wasn't that long ago.
STAN. Where were we?
PRUDENCE. You were trying to keep us from seeing Grandma.
STAN. Oh, yes. You can ask *me* any questions you like, Miss Harper. I know Grandma as well as I do myself.
CHRIS. Maybe even better.
PRUDENCE. *(As* CARL *sits on arm of chair down Right)* When I interview someone, Mr. Nichols, it isn't by proxy. I left New York and a very good cocktail party to fly out here and interview some sacchrin author of children's stories. Either I do that, or I write my opinions starting with one whiskey bottle hidden behind the "Kinsey Report." Do we understand each other?
STAN. But Grandma's heart—
PRUDENCE. If Grandma's heart can stand rushing up

and down stairs the way she did this morning and the general confusion around here, it can stand an interview with Prudence Harper.

CARL. And it doesn't strain a heart to be photographed.

PRUDENCE. Just what are you trying to get away with, Mr. Nichols?

STAN. Nothing at all. Am I, Chris?

CHRIS. This is your idea—keep talking.

HOSKINS. *(Rises and crosses to* STAN*)* Quiet, please, everyone. Now, Mr. Nichols, you must understand that your grandmother is a part of today's America. Her story, her gentle way of speaking must be brought to the American public. We must insist on seeing her if only for a moment. I have been designated by Lawton Ellerbe to present her with a plaque.

STAN. I am well aware of that plaque, but I cannot permit you to see Grandma again this afternoon.

HOSKINS. *(Losing patience)* And I cannot permit Grandma to be kept under lock and key by some third-rate author.

STAN. Third-rate!

MAUDE. *(Comes bustling downstairs done up as Grandma Letty. This time she has a fan which she holds in front of her face. Her eyes peak over it coyly)* My public!

PRUDENCE. Quick, Carl—a picture!

CARL. O.K.

STAN. No! *(Jumps between* MAUDE *and* CARL *and hurries* MAUDE *up the stairs.)*

PRUDENCE. *(To* CARL*)* Did you get it?

CARL. No, that jerk was in the way.

HOSKINS. *(With great despair)* I didn't even give her the plaque.

CHRIS. Gentlemen, please be seated. Since she seems to have recovered, I am sure Grandma will be down again.

STAN. *(Comes down the stairs. He tries to be jovial)* Pardon the interruption.

PRUDENCE. She seemed pretty spry to me.
STAN. Since Grandma feels better and since you insist, she has consented to see each of you separately.
PRUDENCE. Why separately?
STAN. With all of you firing questions at the same time, she'd get confused and wouldn't know what to say.
CHRIS. *(Sits on the Left arm of the sofa)* She gets confused very easily.
STAN. Is that all right with both parties? Mr. Hoskins?
HOSKINS. Fine.
STAN. Miss Harper, Mr. Henderson?
PRUDENCE. All right with us.
STAN. You'll see her for a short time apiece and no pictures.
CARL. But I—
PRUDENCE. *(Squelching* CARL*)* Leave it to me. *(To* STAN*)* Certainly, Mr. Nichols.
STAN. I'll bring her down. Chris, you arrange the interviews.
CHRIS. Thanks.

(STAN *goes upstairs.)*

PRUDENCE. Who's the lucky one to go first?
CHRIS. *(Rises)* It doesn't really make much difference.
HOSKINS. If you let me see her first, Pru, I think you might get a better story. I have some matters to talk over with her that might give you an exceptionally good exclusive.
PRUDENCE. On the other hand, you might get her to keep some secrets from the press.
CHRIS. Mr. Hoskins' telegram came before you arrived, Miss Harper; therefore, he gets priority.
PUDENCE. *Life* bows to the publisher from New York.

HOSKINS. I just want time to talk over a few business matters—you understand.
PRUDENCE. It all goes to Uncle Sam anyway.
CHRIS. Why don't you two go outside and—
PRUDENCE. We know—walk around the garden.
CHRIS. Yes.
PRUDENCE. Isn't it getting a little crowded out there?
CHRIS. It's big enough.
PRUDENCE. Come on, Carl, I want to talk to you. *(To* HOSKINS*)* We'll give you ten minutes, Hoskie.
HOSKINS. Fifteen?
PRUDENCE. Ten! And don't persuade Grandma to hold out any information. I wouldn't like to be disappointed in you. Besides, if I'm double-crossed, I can be pretty much of a stinker in print.
HOSKINS. You'll get all the information. Run along, Louella.
PRUDENCE. Just so we understand each other.

(PRUDENCE *and* CARL *exit French windows.*)

CHRIS. *(Crossing to* HOSKINS*)* Cigarette while we wait?
HOSKINS. Never smoke—my stomach. *(He looks around, sees that no one else is there, crosses to the stairs and looks up them. Then he comes Center)*
(CHRIS. *watches him fascinated.*)
Mrs. Nichols.
CHRIS. Is anything the matter?
HOSKINS. There is something I must tell you.
CHRIS. What is it?
HOSKINS. Let me come over there where we can talk quietly. *(He crosses to* CHRIS*)* I don't want anyone to overhear.
CHRIS. Is it serious?
HOSKINS. Sit here.

(They sit on the sofa.)

CHRIS. Are you all right?

HOSKINS. Wait a minute. *(He takes out his pill box; almost has a pill to his mouth when he decides against it)* No, I'm too nervous to take a pill. *(Puts the box back in his vest pocket.)*

CHRIS. Is something wrong?

HOSKINS. I hardly know how to begin. You see, I'm a very lonely man. I've spent most of my life building up my business. I've devoted all my time, day and night—even weekends. Now, I'm wealthy, famous, and very lonesome.

CHRIS. Lonesome—a personable man like you?

HOSKINS. All alone, Mrs. Nichols. There's nothing for me to do. I read books all day long, so what pleasure is there for me in curling up with a good book at night?

CHRIS. You're too concerned with business—you should take a vacation and travel.

HOSKINS. All alone? No, Mrs. Nichols, but I have found a solution to my problem.

CHRIS. What's that?

HOSKINS. *(Crosses to French windows and draws drapes across them)* I'm going to ask Grandma Letty to marry me!

CHRIS. Mr. Hoskins!

HOSKINS. Don't say anything yet. I want you to know that I've thought it over. She's not exactly the way I'd pictured her. She's larger and not as dainty, but still, at heart, she is the woman I have come to love through her books.

CHRIS. But you can't marry her.

HOSKINS. Why not? I have everything a man can offer. Money, social position, a home in New York and another in Palm Springs.

CHRIS. I mean—well—that is to say, you hardly know one another.

HOSKINS. When you get to be my age, you can tell what a woman is like at the very first meeting.

CHRIS. But Grandma isn't—well, isn't exactly what she seems to be.

HOSKINS. In what way?

CHRIS. Well, she—she's different from most women. (MAUDE *comes down the stairs having taken off the Grandma Letty costume.*)
Maude, I thought you—

MAUDE. No, it seems we don't change horses in midstream.

CHRIS. I see.

MAUDE. I am through with the theatre. Never again.

CHRIS. It's just as well, Maude. The next act is going to be a lulu.

MAUDE. If you need me, just call. *(She goes into the kitchen.)*

HOSKINS. *(Turns to* CHRIS*)* Well, what do you think? Wouldn't you like to get Grandma out from underfoot?

CHRIS. This place wouldn't be the same without her.

HOSKINS. I see what you mean. I suppose your husband does live off her.

CHRIS. *(Indignantly)* He does not.

HOSKINS. What does he do besides attempt to write?

CHRIS. Well, he—he—

HOSKINS. I thought so. You poor, dear child. You must have been very young when you married.

CHRIS. *(Rises angrily)* I was no child bride and I'll not have you making snide remarks about Stanley. He's a wonderful husband and a good provider. Look at the way he supports my niece.

HOSKINS. But he doesn't, Mrs. Nichols—Grandma does.

CHRIS. Listen, Mr. Hoskins— *(Crosses Center and turns)* No, wait a minute. On second thought, go on—propose to Grandma. I think it's a wonderful idea. It will bring a lot of truths out in the open where they should be. By all means, go ahead.

HOSKINS. *(Crosses in towards* CHRIS*)* I'm glad I have your sanction. Tell me, how do you think she'll react?

CHRIS. Violently!

HOSKINS. In the affirmative?
CHRIS. It's hard to say, but don't take "No" for an answer. Use all your persuasive powers.
HOSKINS. Yes. "Damn the torpedoes, full speed ahead!"
CHRIS. That's the idea. I'll be interested in the outcome—very interested indeed.
HOSKINS. But you will leave us alone?
CHRIS. As much as I'd like to stay, I guess it's only polite.
HOSKINS. Thank you, my dear. Wish me luck.
CHRIS. *(Holds out her hand)* Good luck, Mr. Hoskins.

(They shake hands as STAN *comes down the stairs. He has put on the Grandma Letty costume again in one last attempt to straighten things out. His main purpose is to get the plaque and get rid of* HOSKINS.*)*

HOSKINS. *(As he and* CHRIS *shake hands, he sees* STAN*)* Ah, there you are, my dear.
STAN. For a minute. Just time enough to let you give me the plaque, then I must rest.
CHRIS. *(Starts for the kitchen door)* I'd better check with Maude about dinner.
STAN. *(Imploring her)* Don't you want to stay, Christine?
CHRIS. Maude doesn't know what to cook.
HOSKINS. *(Pleased that* CHRIS *is leaving them alone)* Thank you for your help.
CHRIS. You're welcome. Don't forget. *(She gestures straight into the air)* "Damn the torpedoes."
HOSKINS. *(Copies her gesture right in front of* STAN'S *face)* "Full speed ahead!"
CHRIS. Right! *(She goes out.)*
STAN. What's all that mean?
HOSKINS. A private matter.
STAN. Oh—and now for the plaque.

HOSKINS. *(Indicating the sofa)* Sit here, my dear.

STAN. *(Sits on the Left side of the sofa)* There we are— I'm ready.

HOSKINS. *(Stands by the Center side of the sofa)* And now, before I make the presentation, I have a small question to ask you.

STAN. About business, Mr. Hoskins?

HOSKINS. *(Sits on the sofa beside* STAN*)* Call me Cyril!

STAN. *(Giggles coyly)* Cyril.

HOSKINS. There. That's better. *(Pat's* STAN*'s hand.)*

STAN. *(Withdrawing the hand)* Let's not talk business now, Cyril, unless—of course—it's about Stanley's book. You *have* decided to publish it after all.

HOSKINS. Hardly. Letty, that book is a muddled up philosophical study of nothing.

STAN. Muddled up? I thought it extremely clear.

HOSKINS. I'm afraid he doesn't have the clear-cut, charming style with which you're endowed.

STAN. *(Turning away)* I don't think we agree—you and I.

HOSKINS. Now, now, Letty, we mustn't waste our few minutes together. I must talk to you.

STAN. *(Pleasantly)* That's what you're doing, isn't it?

HOSKINS. I mean about a different matter. *(He moves along the sofa towards* STAN.*)*

STAN. *(Sliding away from him)* What matter?

HOSKINS. Us.

STAN. *(Surprised)* Us?

HOSKINS. You and me. Letty, this isn't the life for you—living with your relatives. I can tell you're unhappy. My life, too, is not all it might be. I need companionship, a kindrd spirit who will share my final years with me. Will you bring me life's greatest happiness? Will you bring sunlight into the shade of my life? Letty, will you marry me?

STAN. *What!*

HOSKINS. Say you'll be Letty Hoskins.

STAN. Letty Hos—no—oh, no—you and me! *(He throws his head back and laughs uproariously. Suddenly he realizes what has happened and stops abruptly)* Excuse me.

HOSKINS. *(Bewildered)* Did you understand me?

STAN. Yes, I understood. I'm afraid the surprise was too much for me. I often act that way when the unexpected happens.

HOSKINS. Letty, say you will. I can see us together in the evening, me sitting in front of the fire with my slippers on doing a crossword puzzle. You over in the corner working away on another best-seller, then pattering out to the kitchen and surprising me with some herb tea. And, as I lie in bed at the end of the day, the music of your typewriter keys lulls me to dreamland,

STAN. What a perfect life!

HOSKINS. *(Leaning in to* STAN*)* You will say "Yes," won't you, Letty?

STAN. Don't you feel that—well, that we should think about it for awhile. I hardly know you.

HOSKINS. But I know you so well through your wonderful stories. I'll give you anything your little heart desires—mink coats— Cadillacs—yachts— I'll do anything for you.

STAN. Anything?

HOSKINS. Name it.

STAN. Even publish Stanley's book?

HOSKINS. But, Letty—

STAN. *(Gritting his teeth and going ahead)* It would be a best-seller, Cyril, I know it would.

HOSKINS. You're trying to trifle with my reputation. That book is not worth the merit of a Cyril B. Hoskins' publication.

STAN. *(Pulls* HOSKINS' *hair into a little knot on the top of his head)* Not even if I asked for this itty-bitty favor to show how much you care for Grandma?

HOSKINS. Well—

STAN. Say you will, Cyril. It will make Stanley so happy—launch him on a career all of his own.

HOSKINS. Excuse me, Letty. *(He rises and takes a pill without the aid of water)* I must think this over coldly and sensibly. I'll go over here. *(He crosses to the French windows)* If I'm near you, my emotions carry me away.

STAN. All right. You think about it.

(HOSKINS *is looking out the French windows.* STAN *heaves a big sigh, mops his brow with his sleeves, gets up and crosses Center. He looks at the bookcase and spies the whiskey bottle on the bottom shelf. He glances at* HOSKINS, *sees he is not looking and picks up the bottle. He is in the middle of his first swallow when* HOSKINS *turns around.)*

HOSKINS. *(Shocked at the sight)* Letty!

STAN. *(Chokes on the swallow and sprays it out in front of him. He realizes he is caught and acts on the spur of the moment)* Oh! Oh! My heart! *(He clutches at his heart.)*

HOSKINS. *(Rushes to* STAN, *replaces the bottle and guides* STAN *to the sofa)* There. There. I didn't mean to startle you.

STAN. But you yelled so loud.

HOSKINS. Come and sit down. Rest yourself.

STAN. *(As he sits on the sofa fanning himself with his shawl)* Oh, Cyril, the excitement of the last few minutes has started my palpitations. I have to take a little stimulant every now and then. Doctor's orders.

HOSKINS. Of course, Letty. You poor, dear thing. I'll take you away to the country—to the best specialists in America.

STAN. *(Sighs)* There, I feel better now. These momentary vapors come and go quickly.

HOSKINS. *(Sitting beside* STAN) I'm sorry I frightened you, but the sight of Grandma Letty with a bottle to her lips was too much of a shock. Think of the scandal if Prudence Harper would have seen it, think of the children, think of book sales.

STAN. No wonder you screamed.

Hoskins. Forgive me?

Stan. Of course. And what, dear Cyril, did you decide about Stanley's book?

Hoskins. Letty, you live in a world of children's stories. You understand nothing of the cruel, steely world of business. If I were to publish Stanley's book, I'd be laughed right out of New York.

Stan. You mean the answer is "No"?

Hoskins. Yes.

Stan. You mean "Yes"?

Hoskins. No. It's "No."

Stan. Oh, Cyril, I'm so disappointed in you. I thought you— *(He starts crying loudly and turns away to the Left.)*

Hoskins. Don't cry, Letty. Please don't cry.

Stan. Just one small favor, that's all I ask.

Hoskins. I'm afraid I must remain adamant. A woman's tears must not soften a man's business sense.

Stan. You're heartless. Give me my plaque and go. Henceforth, I shall send my books to another publisher.

Hoskins. Now, Letty, you're just acting on the heat of the moment. *(Getting extremely worried)* Think how Hoskins & Company has treated you.

Stan. No. Give me my plaque and send the other people away. I am returning to my seclusion.

Hoskins. *(Turns Stan around facing him)* I won't let you hide away again, Letty. You belong to the children. You belong to the world. *(He rises above Stan, holding Stan down)* You belong to me!

Stan. Watch yourself, sir.

Hoskins. You will marry me, won't you? Won't you, Letty?

Stan. Definitely not. Now take your hands off me.

(Prudence *and* Carl *enter through the French windows. They see what's going on and* Prudence *signals for* Carl *to get ready to take a picture. This is just the blackmail she can use.)*

Hoskins. I won't. Man must conquer his mate, by

force if necessary. Since the beginning of time it has been that way. Now I, like a cave man—claim my woman.

STAN. Leave me alone or I'll scream.

(PRUDENCE *silently crosses to Center while* CARL *gets himself in position above the sofa to take the picture.*)

HOSKINS. Scream away.
STAN. Stanley will come and knock you down— *(Reverting to his natural voice)* —believe me!
HOSKINS. Who cares? You're mine, Letty, all mine.
PRUDENCE. *(Signals* CARL*)* Now!
CARL. *(With camera poised)* Hold it!

(HOSKINS *and* STAN *look towards the camera and* CARL *takes the picture.*)

HOSKINS. *(Rising from the sofa)* What's the meaning of this?
PRUDENCE. Relax, Hoskie, darling.
HOSKINS. *(Crosses above sofa while* CARL *retreats in front of French windows)* Give me that film.
CARL. Not on your life.
STAN. Cyril, this will ruin me.
HOSKINS. Ruin you? What about me? What about book sales?
STAN. But that picture—
HOSKINS. This is all your fault. Thank heavens I'm a bachelor.
PRUDENCE. *(Pad and pencil poised)* May I quote you?
HOSKINS. *(Crosses Center)* What the devil are you doing sneaking around corners with that camera fiend?
CARL. Who's a camera fiend?
STAN. The man said you were.
HOSKINS. Shut up.

ACT II MORE THAN MEETS THE EYE

STAN. Me?

HOSKINS. No.

PRUDENCE. Who?

HOSKINS. Him. *(Points at* CARL.*)*

PRUDENCE. *(Settles in chair up Right)* Now, Grandma, let's have a nice, straight-from-the-shoulder interview. I want the real dope from hay-ride to Hoskins.

STAN. Am I to sit here and be insulted?

HOSKINS. I'm afraid you are.

STAN. What kind of a man are you?

HOSKINS. *(Losing control and almost yelling)* A blackmailed one, so be quiet!

CHRIS. *(Enters from kitchen)* What's going on in here?

STAN. Everything.

CHRIS. How did things work out, Mr. Hoskins?

HOSKINS. They stink!

CHRIS. Well!

STAN. Chris, you'd better go.

CHRIS. *(Leans on the door jamb)* I'm staying. This looks good.

PRUDENCE. Come on, Grandma, I want the truth or that photograph is page one news from Brooklyn to the Golden Gate.

CHRIS. What photograph?

PRUDENCE. An interesting, if censorable one, Carl just took.

CHRIS. Grandma.

STAN. *(Weakly)* Yes, dear.

CHRIS. I think you'd better tell the truth—all of it and right now.

STAN. You know I can't.

PRUDENCE. Whatever the truth is, I advise you to tell it and quickly.

(PEGGY *enters through the front door.)*
Come on, what's the skeleton?

PEGGY. *(She is very upset)* Excuse me.

STAN. *(Glad to change the subject)* Come right in.

PEGGY. *(Crosses to the Right of* HOSKINS*)* Chris, I've just told Bradley everything.

CHRIS. You shouldn't have done that.

PRUDENCE. *(Exasperated)* Why doesn't someone tell the press everything.

PEGGY. *(Turning to* PRUDENCE*)* This is a private matter.

PRUDENCE. Excuse me.

PEGGY. *(To* CHRIS*)* Bradley doesn't believe me. Is it all right if I bring him in and show him the—er— *(Points to* STAN*)* —facts?

CHRIS. Sure—go ahead.

STAN. Spare me something.

PEGGY. *(Goes out the front door to get* BRADLEY*)* Brad, come in.

CHRIS. *(Almost in tears. To* STAN*)* Have you spared me anything? Four years of this and I'm fed up with it. I want to be an honest woman.

CARL. She ain't married!

CHRIS. Sometimes I wish I weren't.

STAN. *(Trying vainly to make her understand)* Christine, don't ever say that again. Stanley loves you. He's doing his best for you.

CHRIS. *(Breaks into tears and sits in chair down Right)* I wish you could see him now!

PRUDENCE. I haven't understood a word of this conversation for the last five minutes.

PEGGY. *(Brings* BRADLEY *in to Center)* Come on. *(Points to* STAN*)* There, Brad. Look.

BRAD. Holy smoke!

PEGGY. Now, am I lying?

BRAD. *(Staring at* STAN *who writhes uncomfortably)* I can't believe it!

PRUDENCE. Believe what?

BRAD. It can't be.

PRUDENCE. Be what?

PEGGY. Now you know the whole truth. That's the family I come from. That's how smart we are. And I'm

not even as intelligent as that— *(Indicates* STAN*)*
—that creature! *(Starts to cry)* You'd better go.
  BRAD. Peggy, I don't know what to say.
  PEGGY. Just good-bye! *(She runs up the stairs crying.)*
  BRAD. *(Following her to the foot of the stairs)* Peggy!
  STAN. *(Starts to rise)* Chris! *(Sees that she, too, is crying and he sits again.)*

*(*BRAD *goes out, closing the front door after him.)*

  PRUDENCE. Let's start all over.
  HOSKINS. *(Crosses to* PRUDENCE*)* I want that negative.
  PRUDENCE. *(Rises)* I want that interview.
  STAN. What more can happen?

(The front door bursts open and a woman enters. She is MISS JENKINS*, advance woman for United News Service. She is in her thirties, chic, but the type that doesn't easily get ruffled. She has a job to do and she does it, whatever stands in her way.)*

  JENKINS. Here I am!
  PRUDENCE. I might have known you'd show up.
  CARL. You'll have trouble, Jenkins.
  STAN. Who is Jenkins?
  JENKINS. *(Crosses down Center)* I'm the advance girl for United News Service. The cameramen will be here in a few minutes and I get things ready for them.
  STAN. Newsreels—what next?
  JENKINS. *(After surveying the room quickly)* Uh-huh! Now the room isn't quite right. I'll have to change a few things around. Hope you don't mind. *(Crosses to* CHRIS*)* Excuse me. *(Lifts* CHRIS *out of the chair and moves the chair over nearer the bookcase. She is going to make a little setting there for the newsreel cameraman. During the remainder of the scene, she is con-*

stantly on the move making her little set, oblivious of what is going on around her.)

NORA. *(Enters through the French windows with a bunch of roses)* Excuse me, Chris. I didn't know you had company.

(STAN *hides behind his shawl.)*

CHRIS. *(Through her tears)* You might as well come in and join the circus.
NORA. *(Crosses below the sofa to Center)* You're crying.
CHRIS. Uh-huh.
NORA. What's the matter?
PRUDENCE. We'd all like to know.
NORA. I remember you. You're the one who thought I was Chris.
PRUDENCE. And you're the neighborly neighbor dropping by with roses.
STAN. Roses!
HOSKINS. *(Charging on* NORA *and taking the roses)* I am Cyril B. Hoskins—give me those.
NORA. Hey, those aren't yours.
HOSKINS. I need them.
JENKINS. *(Having finished her first project, she now heads for the French windows to fix the drapes, but* NORA *is in her way, so she pushes* NORA *upstage)* Excuse me.
NORA. Who's that?
STAN. Oh—someone.
NORA. Thanks. *(For the first time she sees* STAN*)* Oh, you look good. You'll win the prize Saturday night.
PRUDENCE. Here we go again. More mumbo-jumbo.
HOSKINS. Carl, here's a picture for you. *(As he dumps the flowers into* STAN'S *lap)* Hold these flowers.
STAN. But they're roses.
HOSKINS. I know they're roses. Carl, wait until I

get the plaque. *(He picks up the plaque and stands by* STAN *to the Left of the sofa.)*
  JENKINS. *(Decides, after straightening the drapes, that she needs* STAN'S *shawl to put over the chair she originally moved. So she takes it from* STAN'S *shoulders)* Excuse me.
  STAN. *(Fighting back the sneezes brought on by the roses)* Chris! Chris, help me!
  CHRIS. You brought it on yourself, Granny.
  PRUDENCE. Are you ready, Carl?

(STAN *sneezes.)*

  CARL. *(In position down Left)* Hold it, Grandma.
  STAN. *(Sneezes)* Roses!
  MAUDE. *(Enters from the kitchen on the last sneeze)* Gesundheit!
  JENKINS. *(Arranging the table down Right, she finds* MAUDE *in her way and pushes her downstage)* Excuse me.
  HOSKINS. *(To* STAN*)* What's the matter with you?
  STAN. Roses, that's what!
  PRUDENCE. *(Coming in Center and regarding* STAN*)* Roses! But Stanley told me he was the only one who— Stanley told me— *(Points at him)* Stanley!
  STAN. No! *(He sneezes)* Quiet! Don't!

(PRUDENCE *runs to the telephone.)*

  HOSKINS. What's going on?
  STAN. *(Rises and starts to cross to the phone, but* CARL *stops him Left of sofa)* Somebody stop her! *(He sneezes again.)*
  PRUDENCE. *(Into the phone)* Long distance—hurry!
  NORA. What's the matter?
  CHRIS. Everything!
  STAN. No, Miss Harper!
  PRUDENCE. Get me *Life Magazine,* New York City. This will make me another Marguerite Higgins.

STAN. *(Crosses to below the sofa)* What will I do? What's left for me to do?
MAUDE. Do what you told me.
STAN. What?
MAUDE. When all else fails—remember? *(She puts her hand to her forehead.)*
STAN. Oh!
PRUDENCE. Operator, hurry the call!
STAN. My heart! Oh, my heart! *(He faints onto the sofa amid the roses.)*
JENKINS. *(Seeing the roses, she has decided these are the ideal things for the setting. As* HOSKINS *goes to bend over* STAN, *she pushes him aside)* Excuse me, *(She is picking up the roses as*

THE CURTAIN FALLS

ACT THREE

It is a short time later. The room is about the same, the drapes are open, but the French doors are closed. NORA is pacing up and downstage by the French windows. PRUDENCE is pacing up and down Center. MAUDE is standing by the kitchen door, a belligerent look on her face.

PRUDENCE. *(Stops her pacing momentarily)* But why would—
MAUDE. Mr. Hoskins said to keep quiet or you'll disturb Grandma.

(PRUDENCE *resumes pacing.*)

NORA. *(After a pause)* This Grandma business. I'd like to—
MAUDE. Didn't you hear me?
NORA. I'd just like to know what's going on in this madhouse.
MAUDE. Shh!
PRUDENCE. *(She and NORA pace again in silence)* Why would he?
NORA. Why would who?
MAUDE. *(Coming to a decision)* That settles it. *(She goes into the kitchen.)*
PRUDENCE. Why would someone not admit to being famous when they are? Why would they keep it a secret?
NORA. *(Mystified)* Who?
PRUDENCE. Let's not beat about the bush, darling. You live next door. Don't try to make me believe you don't know about the double life over here.

NORA. *(Crosses below the sofa)* Double life? All I know is this was a very nice quiet town this morning and this was a peaceful home. Now look at it! What's happened?
PRUDENCE. You honestly don't know?
NORA. *(Sits on the Left end of the sofa with her chin in her hands)* I don't know a thing and it's very frustrating.
PRUDENCE. Who'd believe it—even the neighbors don't know. This is a better kept secret than the atom bomb.
NORA. But why is Stanley—
MAUDE. *(Enters clutching a large frying pan. She crosses Center)* I hate to say it, but if you two don't keep quiet, I'm going into action.
PRUDENCE. *(Backs up to the sofa)* All right, I've found out all I want to know.
NORA. I haven't found out a thing.
MAUDE. Now sit down and be quiet until Mr. Hoskins says what's to be done.

(PRUDENCE *sits besides* NORA *on the sofa.* MAUDE *stands above them with frying pan held menacingly. They sit in silence.* PRUDENCE *offers* NORA *a cigarette.* NORA *takes it, mouths the words, "Thank you."* PRUDENCE *takes one and looks for a match.* NORA *lights both cigarettes with match from coffee table.* PRUDENCE *mouths "Thank you." They puff simultaneously.* NORA *inspects* PRUDENCE'S *suit and mouths "I like it."* PRUDENCE *smiles and mouths "Thank you."* NORA *tries to indicate to* PRUDENCE *that she would like to know where* PRUDENCE *bought it. She tries pantomime, then mouthing the words, but gives up.* PRUDENCE *gets her pencil and pad and hands them to* NORA. *She looks at* MAUDE *and writes "Where did you buy it?"* MAUDE *leans over her shoulder watching.* PRUDENCE *reads the note and says, "Oh!"* MAUDE *raises the frying pan and the* TWO WOMEN *duck.*

ACT III MORE THAN MEETS THE EYE

(PRUDENCE *shows* NORA *the label from the neck of the suit. They* BOTH *sit smoking in silence.* HOSKINS *comes down the stairs quietly. He mops his brow with his handkerchief.*)

HOSKINS. Thank you for being so quiet.

(ALL THREE *in the room jump.*)

MAUDE. I kept them that way.
PRUDENCE. *(Rises)* What's the latest?
HOSKINS. *(Crosses down Right)* I don't know. Peggy is in there with Grandma now. Mrs. Nichols seemed rather annoyed and locked herself in her room—strangest attitude to take.
CARL. *(Comes downstairs and crosses Center)* That dame's a heavyweight. She's solid.
NORA. *(At the point of exasperation)* Would someone please take a few minutes off to tell me the whole story— I'd be very grateful.
CARL. Who knows the story? Did you make your call, Pru?
PRUDENCE Hoskins wouldn't let me. And now I'm just as glad he didn't.
CARL. Why?
PRUDENCE. *(Crosses to French windows)* No one else can get the story, can they?
CARL. I shouldn't think so.
PRUDENCE. So I'm going to wait, get all the facts, and make this the biggest story since the Chicago fire. I have another picture for you to take.
CARL. Of what?
PRUDENCE. Come out here.
(They start to go out the French windows.)
I'm going to drop a bombshell in a certain person's lap and I want a picture of his face when that bomb explodes. Here's the story—

(They are out of sight.)

NORA. *(Raises clasped hands)* Maude— Mr. Hoskins, will one of you tell me what all this excitement is about?

HOSKINS. *(Looking after* PRUDENCE *and* CARL*)* Later, my dear. Later.

NORA. *(Rises and crosses Center)* If you won't tell me, then I'm going upstairs and ask Chris.

HOSKINS. She's locked her door.

NORA. She'll talk to *me*.

MAUDE. Ask her if she wants me to do anything.

NORA. The first thing I ask is a reasonable explanation of the last two hours starting with those reporters. *(She goes upstairs.)*

HOSKINS. For a prying neighbor, she doesn't seem to understand very much.

MAUDE. Who does?

HOSKINS. At least the newsreel is out of our hair for a few hours.

MAUDE. That Jenkins lady said she'd check back later. What then?

HOSKINS. If Grandma has recovered, all well and good, but we're not taking chances with such a frail old lady.

MAUDE. She ain't frail.

HOSKINS. Fainting like that— I wouldn't call her strong.

MAUDE. She's as strong as Mr. Nichols.

HOSKINS. By the way, where is that spineless weakling?

MAUDE. *(Crosses in Center)* He ain't no weakling.

HOSKINS. *(Crosses to* MAUDE*)* But where is he? Was he down here protecting his home from the intrusion of reporters? No. Did he help us when Grandma fainted? No.

MAUDE. When he works, he don't hear a thing.

HOSKINS. *(Crosses to the foot of the stairs)* I think I'd better go up and see how Grandma is.

MAUDE. *(Following him)* I wouldn't advise that.

HOSKINS. It's time someone did something. I've a

good mind to call a specialist to fly out here and look at Grandma.

(NORA *comes downstairs.*)

MAUDE. Well, Mrs. Ramson?
NORA. I made a bargain.
HOSKINS. With whom?
NORA. With Chris. If I take those reporters over to my house for half an hour, then she says we'll get an explanation.
HOSKINS. What kind of an explanation?
NORA. *(As she crosses to the French windows)* Of the last two hours, that's what. *(Calls)* Miss Harper.
PRUDENCE. *(Offstage)* Yes.
NORA. *(As she goes out)* I'd like to see you a minute.

(MAUDE *follows* NORA *to the French windows as* NORA *exits.*)

HOSKINS. That woman is exceedingly dumb.
MAUDE. She might know more than you think. *(Looks out French windows)* Good, they're talking. There they go into Mrs. Ramson's house. Well, that settles them for awhile.
HOSKINS. *(Crosses into room)* Something's peculiar—it's not like Pru to desert the battleground.
MAUDE. Clever, that's what it is. She's trading a half an hour away from here for a complete explanation. Besides, she knows more than you think.
HOSKINS. Knows about what?
MAUDE. Just knows.
HOSKINS. I don't have time for double-talk. I'm going to phone that heart specialist right now. It's time for some action. *(Crosses to the phone.)*
MAUDE. *(Follows* HOSKINS*)* Don't, please. Grandma has had these attacks before. They pass quickly.
HOSKINS. She needs a specialist.
MAUDE. She's all right.

HOSKINS. *(Into phone)* Operator, I want long distance.

STAN. *(Offstage upstairs knocking on door)* Chris! Chris! Open the door and let me in.

CHRIS. *(Upstairs)* No.

HOSKINS. *(Into phone)* I want to place a long distance call to Dr. Samuel Tessendorf, Park Avenue, New York City.

MAUDE. *(Calls upstairs)* Mr. Nichols.

STAN. *(Upstairs)* What?

MAUDE. You better come down here.

STAN. *(Upstairs)* I can't.

MAUDE. You must, Mr. Nichols. This is trouble.

STAN. I have trouble enough up here.

HOSKINS. *(Into phone)* Operator, please hurry.

MAUDE. Oh, dear. *(Runs up the stairs calling as she goes)* Mr. Nichols. Mr. Nichols.

HOSKINS. Damn telephone. It's quicker by carrier pigeon. *(Into phone)* Yes, I'm still waiting.

STAN. *(Upstairs)* What!

HOSKINS. *(Into phone)* Dr. Tessendorf, please

STAN. *(Running down the stairs)* No— No— No!

HOSKINS. *(Into phone)* Hello, Dr. Tessendorf, this is—

STAN. *(Clamps his hand over the receiver)* Stop, Mr. Hoskins.

HOSKINS. *(Still holding onto the phone)* So you've come out of hiding. Will you please let go of that phone?

STAN. *(Coming to Left of* HOSKINS. *They* BOTH *still have hold of the phone)* Listen to me.

HOSKINS. What is the meaning of this?

STAN. That's my phone and I won't have you making long distance calls on it.

HOSKINS. I'll pay you.

STAN. When?

HOSKINS. *(Furiously)* I don't know when. Give me that phone.

STAN. If you'll just be patient a minute and listen—

ACT III MORE THAN MEETS THE EYE

Hoskins. All right. What is it?
Stan. Grandma is much better. In fact, she's completely recovered. She's had these fainting spells before, the doctor knows all about them.
Hoskins. She ought to be looked after.
Stan. Peggy's looking after her right now.
Hoskins. I mean by a specialist.
Stan. She's been to the best in the country. They gave her some powders to take. Why, she looks just fine.
Hoskins. *(Starts up the stairs)* I want to see for myself.
Stan. *(Replaces phone on hook)* You can't do that!
Hoskins. Why not if she's so much better?
Stan. She has to rest after these attacks. Always two hours with no noise.
Hoskins. *(Tiptoes back into the room and talks in a whisper)* Oh, then we must be quiet.
Stan. That's why I was trying to stop you from phoning.
Hoskins. *(At Center)* Oh, I see.
Stan. *(Playing along with* Hoskins, *he whispers, too)* Now let's sit down and have a drink.
Hoskins. Not that crush stuff?
Stan. No—whiskey. *(Crosses to bottle on bottom shelf of bookcase.)*
Hoskins. I shouldn't—my stomach. Why, I haven't tasted a drop in over thirty years.
Stan. Then a little shot will be good for you. *(There is no glass and* Stan *pours a shot in a small vase by the bottle.)*
Hoskins. But my doctors—oh, the hell with it.
Stan. Good for you. *(Crosses to* Hoskins*)* There. Shall we drink to Grandma Letty?
Hoskins. *(Toasting)* Grandma Letty.
    (Stan *toasts with the bottle but does not drink.)* Oh, that's good. I'd forgotten how it warms all the way down.

STAN. Peggy said Nora had taken the others to her house.

HOSKINS. *(Crosses and sits Left end of sofa)* Yes, they're supposed to stay there for half an hour on the guarantee of some sort of explanation of something.

STAN. *(Crosses to* HOSKINS*)* Half an hour? Miss Harper will never keep quiet that long.

HOSKINS. Yes, she will. She said no other reporter could get the story so she was going to wait until she knew everything.

STAN. Here—let me give you another. *(Takes the glass.)*

HOSKINS. She did seem very excited just before your grandmother fainted. She said she should have known all the time—something about Grandma and the roses and you.

STAN. Me?

HOSKINS. Yes, she mentioned your name.

STAN. *(Fighting for time, he gives* HOSKINS *the glass)* Here.

HOSKINS. I shouldn't really, but my stomach does feel better after that last one. These confounded doctors don't know what they're talking about. *(Toasting)* To more and better books from Grandma. *(He drinks)* Yes, sir, she mentioned your name.

STAN. That's all she said about me?

HOSKINS. That's all about *you*, but just now, as she went out, she said something about dropping a bombshell in someone's lap— I think she meant mine.

STAN. *(As he sits Right on sofa, to himself)* Then she does know.

HOSKINS. Know what?

STAN. *(Laughs weakly to cover up)* Know whatever she knows?

HOSKINS. *(The whiskey is beginning to show. Not having any in over thirty years and then consuming several straight shots makes its mark)* Anyway, Carl is supposed to take a picture whenever what she knows comes out in the open.

STAN. *(Takes* HOSKINS' *glass)* I just hope they stay at Nora's a long time.
HOSKINS. Yes, we mustn't have any noise. *(Starts whispering again)* I forgot.
STAN. *(Also whispering)* Here. *(Gives back the glass with another shot.)*
HOSKINS. *(The whole world looks brighter)* Thanks, my boy. *(Drinks)* You know, Stanley, I misjudged you.
STAN. Really?
HOSKINS. Uh-hum. You're not a bad sort at all.
STAN. Have you decided you misjudged my book?
HOSKINS. That book! *(Laughs)* Oh, that was terrible—awful! *(Laughs again, then looks around him and whispers again)* Shh! We must be quiet. I'm surprised at you. Don't make so much noise.
STAN. I won't.
HOSKINS. *(Continues whispering)* See that you don't. Another little one?
STAN. *(Taking* HOSKINS' *glass)* Sure—anything to oblige.
HOSKINS. *(Puts his arm around* STAN) Yes, my boy, you and I are going to be very good friends. You may even be my grandson.

(MAUDE *enters and comes down the stairs.)*

STAN. What an honor. *(Hands back the glass.)*
HOSKINS. Yes, I suppose it is. *(Drinks.)*
MAUDE. *(Comes Center. She picks up the whispering)* What shall I do about dinner?
STAN. *(Still whispering)* I don't know—make some coffee or something.
MAUDE. All right. *(She starts to go into the kitchen.)*
HOSKINS. She's a lovely person.
MAUDE. *(Turns)* Thanks. Why are we whispering?
STAN. Grandma's resting—no noise.
MAUDE. Oh. *(Starts to go through the door, then*

realizes what STAN *has said, turns and gives him a disgusted look and goes out.)*

HOSKINS. *(Confidentially)* You're very fortunate to have such a lovely person for a domestic.

STAN. Thank you.

HOSKINS. *(Pats* STAN'S *head)* And she has such lovely employers.

STAN. They aren't bad. *(He puts the bottle on the coffee table.)*

HOSKINS. In fact everyone's lovely. *(Laughs warmly.)*

STAN. *(Crosses to the phone and starts dialing)* Even you, Mr. Hoskins.

HOSKINS. I'm the loveliest of them all.

STAN. Help yourself to another.

HOSKINS. Lovely. *(He drinks from the bottle.)*

STAN. *(Into phone)* Nora? Stan. I'm sending another one over— Hoskins. He needs some strong, black coffee— Please, Nora. Is Harper behaving herself? She's waiting, huh? Good. I'll meet you at the hedge. *(He hangs up.)*

HOSKINS. *(Stroking the bottle)* Lovely bottle. Lovely l-label. *(He pats it.)*

STAN. *(Crossing down to* HOSKINS) Mr. Hoskins.

HOSKINS. Lovely sofa. Lovely cushions. *(Slaps the sofa and dust flies out. Delighted)* Ohh, lovely dust.

STAN. And you're going to take a lovely walk.

HOSKINS. A walk?

STAN. Across the yard and next door. Come along. (STAN *guides him to French windows)* It will do you good. A lovely walk, some lovely black coffee, and then you won't feel quite so lovely.

HOSKINS. *(As they disappear)* Oh, lovely day— lovely garden—

(After a pause, the front DOORBELL rings. MAUDE *enters from the kitchen and opens the door.* BRADLEY *is there.)*

BRAD. Hello, Maude—is Peggy in?
MAUDE. *(Starts to whisper)* I think— *(Realizes her stupidity and talks in normal voice)* I think so.
BRAD. Don't you know?
MAUDE. I wouldn't be sure of anything today. It's been hard to keep track of who is who and who is where.
BRAD. I'd like to see Mr. Nichols first.
MAUDE. He was here a minute ago.
STAN. *(As he enters)* Another out of the way, Maude. Oh, hello, Brad.
BRAD. Hello, sir.
MAUDE. *(To* BRADLEY*)* Do you want me to call Peggy?
BRAD. No, thank you. *(Crosses down Center)* I'll finish with Mr. Nichols first.
MAUDE. Have it your own way. *(She goes into the kitchen.)*
STAN. *(Having had about enough, he flops onto the sofa)* Finish with me? Not now, Brad— I've been told off by too many people in too short a time. I can't take any more.
BRAD. I'm not going to tell you off— I wouldn't dare do that. I just want to apologize for my behavior this afternoon.
STAN. *(Surprised)* Apologize?
BRAD. I just didn't understand, that's all.
STAN. I don't see how you could have misunderstood. It was obvious enough.
BRAD. I understood all right, but I didn't realize the deeper meaning. You see, something happened after I left here and, with your permission, I'd like to call you "sir" again.
STAN. You can call me anything you like as long as it makes you happy.
BRAD. Thank you, sir. And now I have something to straighten out with Peggy.
STAN. Would you like me to call her?

BRAD. If you don't mind.
STAN. *(Crosses to foot of stairs)* It's nice to see somebody's problems being talked over sensibly. *(Calls upstairs)* Peggy.
PEGGY. *(Upstairs)* Yes.
STAN. Bradley is down here.
PEGGY. *(Upstairs)* Tell him to go away.
STAN. He wants to talk to you— I think he's going to apologize.
PEGGY. *(Upstairs. Brightly)* I'll be right down.
STAN. *(Comes back into the room)* I don't know why it's easier to settle problems *before* marriage.
BRAD. Is it?
STAN. Much. But then, if it weren't easier, people wouldn't get married and what would that make us?
BRAD. Sir!
STAN. I mean, we wouldn't be here, would we?
BRAD. I guess not. *(As he sees* PEGGY *coming down the stairs)* Hi!
PEGGY. Hi!
STAN. *(Crossing to the stairs)* I'm in the way so I'll go upstairs and try a new attack on my own battle line.
PEGGY. The door is still locked and I don't blame Chris.
STAN. You women certainly stick together.
BRAD. Thank you, sir, for everything.
STAN. Good luck on your talk. Let me know your secret sometime. *(He goes upstairs.)*
BRAD. *(Crosses below the chair up Right)* Peggy, I have something to say.
PEGGY. *(Crosses above sofa)* What is it?
BRAD It's hard for a man to apologize.
PEGGY. *(Softening)* It's hard for anyone.
BRAD. But when a man is wrong and sees the light, it's his duty to swallow his pride and admit he's wrong.
PEGGY. Yes.
BRAD. Well— I was wrong, I'm swallowing and I apologize. There!

PEGGY. *(Starts to cry)* Bradley. Oh, Bradley.
BRAD. What's the matter?
PEGGY. You weren't wrong.
BRAD. *(Crosses to* PEGGY*)* But I was.
PEGGY. You were right—very right. I've known it all along. *(Cries harder.)*
BRAD. *(Handing her his handkerchief)* Here.
PEGGY. Thanks. *(Blows her nose violently.)*
BRAD. Stop crying—please.
PEGGY. All right. *(Blows again)*
   (BRAD *puts out his hand for the handkerchief.)* (PEGGY *almost gives it to him, then takes it back again)* No, I'll wash it.
BRAD. You're so thoughtful.
PEGGY. *(Faces front)* Bradley, you thought you were wrong and you behaved like a man and I appreciate it. Now I must behave like a sensible woman and not be carried away by—by my feeling for you.
BRAD. Peggy— *(Makes a move to kiss her but she slips away down Left.)*
PEGGY. No, Bradley, it's gone beyond that. You have to listen to me—from over there. *(She indicates the chair down Right.)*
BRAD. Why can't I stay here?
PEGGY. Because I might be carried away—over there, please.
   (BRADLEY *slowly crosses the room and sits down.)* Thank you.
BRAD. Now what is it?
PEGGY. It's just that this afternoon was only a climax to a whole situation that's been brewing for a long time.
BRAD. You mean us?
   (PEGGY *nods.)*
I apologized—what more can I do?
PEGGY. It's not you. It's me. I'm so different from you.
BRAD. What's that got to do with—

PEGGY. You've got to be quiet and stop interrupting. This is very difficult to say.

BRAD. All right, but I—all right.

PEGGY. *(Crosses below sofa)* Let me try to explain. You know how—in chemistry class—we take an article and break it down into its different parts? Well, if I broke us down and put both of us into individual test tubes, do you know what I'd find?

(BRAD *starts to speak but Peggy silences him.*)
I'd find almost all of the same things in each test tube —skin and livers, stuff like that. But I'd also find intangible things like thinking and hearing and feeling. They'd be *almost* the same in each test tube. *(She crosses Center)* But there is one element that your test tube is loaded with that just rattles around in mine. In every other respect we're alike but this one element makes us so different that, if you poured the two test tubes together, they'd never mix. That one element is intelligence. It's too bad but that's the way it is. You're intelligent and I'm not. I didn't think it would make any difference but I know now that it does. If we continued going together—who knows?—we might even get—get married one day and then there would be a family. You'd be a great man in physics or atomic energy or law or something. You'd come home in the evening and I'd never be able to help you or talk about your work with you because I wouldn't understand it. *(She gets herself so worked up, she is about to cry)* Then you'd start finding happiness with other women and we'd get divorced and there would be a big scandal and we'd fight over the custody of the children and,— who wants to keep going together if it will ruin the lives of little children! *(She wails.)*

BRAD. *(Rises and crosses in a few steps, deeply moved).* That was the most beautiful speech I've ever heard. It was better even than the Gettysburg Address. Only it isn't true.

PEGGY. *(Sinks onto the sofa)* You know it is. Why,

I'm not even on the same plane with you. You might as well be on Mars while I'm right here on Earth.

BRAD. *(Crosses to* PEGGY*)* That's just the point, Peggy. You're right here *down* to earth while I'm flying around maybe lost in the fog somewhere. You're my radar, that's what you are.

PEGGY. *(Looking up tearfully)* Am I?

BRAD. *(Sits beside her on the sofa)* Sure. You bring me back to earth safely. If it wasn't for you, heaven knows what would happen to me flying around deep in thought with ceiling zero. Every great man needs a sensible, ordinary woman behind him to keep his feet planted right in the family home. Why we're a wonderful pair. What one of us lacks, the other has.

(PEGGY *looks at him.)*

Oh, I don't mean just that I'm a genius and you're normal. I mean—well—you have compensations.

PEGGY. *(Hoping to be convinced)* What compensations?

BRAD. You can cook and sew and all those little domestic things.

PEGGY. Better than you?

BRAD. I can't even thread a needle or defrost food.

PEGGY. Honest?

BRAD. Uh-huh.

PEGGY. Then together, in one test tube, we make a whole complete unit?

BRAD. That's right. Apart, we're nothing, but together—oh, brother! *(He kisses her.)*

PEGGY. That's the first time you ever kissed me.

BRAD. I know— I liked it. Intelligence doesn't matter a hang when it comes to necking. *(He starts to kiss her again.)*

PEGGY. *(Stopping him)* No. There's too much trouble in this house for us to be so happy.

BRAD. You mean about your Uncle Stanley?

PEGGY. It's a mess. Chris isn't speaking to him, reporters are waiting next door at Nora's house and he won't tell them the truth.

BRAD. Why doesn't Chris tell them?
PEGGY. Chris says if it doesn't come from Stanley, it's no good.
BRAD. It's terrible that something like this should happen to such a wonderful man.
PEGGY. Who?
BRAD. Your uncle, of course.
PEGGY. You can say that after what you saw and heard this afternoon?
BRAD. *(Rises and crosses Center)* It's what happened after I left here that changed my mind.
PEGGY. What did happen?
BRAD. *(Crosses above the sofa and to the Right)* Do you know where I went? To the public library and sat down and looked through "Grandma Letty and The Gruffy Giraffe."
PEGGY. You did that just for me?
BRAD. *(Crosses behind sofa)* You know what—it's great! Honestly it is. It brings out a moral through the animals and, in its own way—it's beautiful.
PEGGY. You really think so?
BRAD. I know so. Imagine me sitting in the children's division of the library and being spellbound by a kid's book. But I was and only because it was too good to put down. You figure it out.
PEGGY. *(Amazed)* I can't.
BRAD. It's because he's more intelligent than all of us put together. It's because he can make anyone pay attention to him—that's a great talent. Peggy, I dare say you are living under the same roof with a genius.
PEGGY. Golly, I never thought of it that way.
STAN. *(Comes down the stairs)* Things remain as they were. I can't get to see the opposition.
BRAD. Maybe you'd better try a new offensive.
STAN. Can't—door's locked.
BRAD. Come on, Peggy, let's go for a drive.
PEGGY. I'd love to but I'd better stay here. They may need some help.

STAN. *(Crossing down)* Thanks, but we'll manage. I don't know how, but we will.

PEGGY. I'm not leaving this house— I've got some interests to protect here. I have a famous Uncle.

STAN. You're proud of me now?

PEGGY. Am I ever!

STAN. You change quickly. What did you use, Brad—hypnosis?

BRAD. The truth, sir.

PEGGY. *(Rises and crosses to BRADLEY)* You run along, Brad. I'll call you when things get settled one way or another.

BRAD. *(Crosses to front door)* O.K. Good luck, Mr. Nichols, sir.

STAN. Thanks.

BRAD. *(Opens the door. To PEGGY)* Don't forget to call.

PEGGY. I won't.

BRAD. *(To STAN)* Take care of Peggy. I need her. She's my radar. *(He goes out.)*

(PEGGY *closes the door and leans against it, facing front.*)

STAN. What did he mean by that?

PEGGY. We have reached an understanding, that's all.

STAN. Peggy, how can I get Chris to talk to me? I've only been trying to protect her, too—you know that. I only did it so she'd be proud of me as an adult writer, as a man to be respected.

PEGGY. *(Crosses down)* I think she's too upset about this afternoon to think clearly right at the moment.

STAN. Those idiots at Nora's will be back soon. I've got to tell them something. I must see Chris and talk to her.

PEGGY. Suppose I go upstairs and tell her someone is down here to see her? Nora, for instance. She'd come down, wouldn't she?

STAN. She'd ask Nora up.

PEGGY. Leave it to me. *(She starts up the stairs)* I have my feet planted firmly on the ground. I have a new found intelligence. *(She goes out.)*

(STAN *crosses to the foot of the stairs and listens.*)

PEGGY. *(Knocking on door upstairs)* Chris.

CHRIS. *(Off)* Yes, Peggy.

PEGGY. *(Off)* Nora's downstairs—it's awful. You'd better come.

Chris. *(Off)* What's happened?

PEGGY. *(Off)* I can't believe it— I just can't.

CHRIS. *(Off stage door opens and her voice gets nearer)*
   (STAN *crosses to below the bookcase so he is not visible from the foot of the stairs.*)
Peggy, is Nora all right?

PEGGY. *(Off)* You'd better go see.

CHRIS. *(Rushes downstairs and crosses to above sofa)* Nora. Nora, what is it?

STAN. *(Crosses and stands below the stairs blocking her path up them again)* It isn't Nora.

CHRIS. You mean— *(Turns)* Oh, Stan, that wasn't fair.

STAN. I had to talk to you.

CHRIS *(Calling up the stairs over* STAN's *shoulder)* Peggy, I'll speak to you about this later.

PEGGY. *(Off)* Go to it, Stan!

CHRIS. Go to it! What made her change sides? What did you do to her?

STAN. Nothing. She saw the light.

CHRIS. *(Crosses close to* STAN) I should like to go to my room if you don't mind.

STAN. *(Spreads his arms out across the stairs)* I do mind.

CHRIS. Don't stand there like Paul Bunyon. You'll have to move sooner or later.

STAN. Not until you listen to me.

ACT III MORE THAN MEETS THE EYE

CHRIS. I suppose you'll keep me down here by force if necessary?

STAN. Isn't that being a little juvenile?

CHRIS. *(Crosses down to above the Center sofa)* I should like to know just what you consider juvenile. I should think dressing up in a wig and cavorting all over the furniture with an elderly admirer would cover it.

STAN. *(Follows her down)* Not if there were a sufficiently adult reason behind it.

CHRIS. I'm not going to stand here and argue with you.

STAN. Then sit down and listen to me. After all, this is a democracy and I have a right to be heard.

CHRIS. A democracy? I'd like to put a few things to a vote like your telling the truth to Mr. Hoskins.

STAN. If you'd just wait and let me explain everything.

CHRIS. *(Sits on the Right arm of the sofa facing front)*

(STAN *is slightly above her.*)
Explain away.

STAN. Well—it seems to me, I've just been trying to protect my home and my business. That's an American man's privilege, isn't it?

CHRIS. Go on—keep explaining.

STAN. I admit I may have gone to some extreme lengths, but it was for us—for you and me.

CHRIS. *(Rises and crosses Center. She turns on* STAN*)* Just a minute—don't drag me into it. Even when your first story was published, I wanted you to tell the truth.

STAN. You know why I didn't. But all this is beside the point. I've come up with a solution to the entire matter. All we have to do is kill Grandma!

CHRIS. What?

STAN. We'll say she died—that will settle everything.

CHRIS. *(Takes a step back)* Stanley!

STAN. *(Pleased with his idea, he sits on the back of the sofa as he thinks it out)* Or better still, I'll send

Hoskins a letter saying Grandma has given up writing and gone away on a trip around the world. Then, if we ever need some more money, I'll say Grandma mailed in a story from a distant port of call. How's that?

CHRIS. *(Shocked)* You'd do that? You'd kill a kind old lady just to get out of this mess?

STAN. You can't kill someone who doesn't live.

CHRIS. But she does live in the hearts of thousands of little children. She lives for me. She's always been as much a part of this household as any of us.

STAN. You're getting carried away with the whole *idea* of Grandma Letty.

CHRIS. *(Crosses in Center)* I'm carried away with an idea—with love for someone who isn't materially here, yes. But I'm not as carried away physically as you've been all day. I wish you could have seen yourself this afternoon. Do you realize you're married to me and practically engaged to someone else?

STAN. Don't try to be funny.

CHRIS. *(Crosses away down Right)* I don't feel funny.

STAN. I've gone on writing Grandma for you. Now I'm willing to kill her for you. What more do you want?

CHRIS. I want an honest husband.

STAN. *(Really stunned by this. He now realizes how serious CHRIS is. He rises and crosses to her speaking quietly)* That's what I'm trying to give you. Honestly, I don't understand you lately—running away from me and locking yourself in your room. We used to be able to talk things over like sensible people.

CHRIS. I find it difficult to talk things over sensibly when every time I turn around you're someone else.

STAN. *(Turns her to face him)* You mean the only reason you're upset is just because I impersonated Grandma Letty?

CHRIS. That's only part of it.

STAN. But you helped me all through it. You played up to Grandma. Why, if you didn't approve?

CHRIS. It was funny for awhile. Besides, I never thought you'd get away with it for so long. How did I know it would take on such monstrous proportions?

STAN. It just grew— I couldn't help it.

CHRIS. *(Crosses below* STAN *to the Center of the sofa)* I realized if I were suddenly to stop the whole thing, whip off your wig and expose you, it wouldn't do any good. You have to *want* to tell the truth. That's always been the answer—from the beginning—from the time we were married.

STAN. *(Crosses towards her)* Chris, you don't mean you're upset about the whole marriage? Why, we've gotten along famously.

CHRIS. I know we've gotten along, but I have to have more than that. I love you, but I have to have more than that, too. You see, Stanley, I don't know if I respect you—if I've ever respected you. I married you in good faith that you were an honest man and that together we would establish a home and something of a normal life. Oh, I knew you were a budding writer, but I'd have starved with you, lived in five-flight walks-ups. I didn't care—as long as we were together, working together for a common goal, that would have been all right with me. But what happens? Right away you sell a story.

STAN. Before we ever had to starve together.

CHRIS. When the first contract came in from Hoskins, I thought you were going to put your name on the cover of the book. But not you. You signed the first book "Grandma Letty" to attract more attention from the public. Maybe it did, I don't know. But you didn't want your real name attached to it—what would happen when you became another Shakespeare?

STAN. That was right, wasn't it?

CHRIS. *(Turns away from* STAN*)* I don't know and I don't think I care any more. The whole point is I'm afraid I'm married to a mouse and not a man.

STAN. I don't understand. I thought you believed in me—had faith in me.

CHRIS. Faith in you! *(She turns)* I'd have swum across the Red Sea with my hands tied behind my back if you'd asked me to.

STAN. *(Crosses to her)* Then why won't you go along with me, stick with it a little longer. I'll be a good author. I know I will.

CHRIS. But you are a good author. You're a great author, don't you see that? You've written a series of books that have made their mark upon people. If you want fame, you've got it. *(Points out French windows)* Right over there is proof of it—magazines, newsreels, plaques, all waiting for you to give the word. If you want money, you've got that, too. After this publicity, you'll be able to retire. Stanley, just what do you want?

STAN. I want you.

CHRIS. *(Almost crying)* Oh, Stan, that was low.

STAN. *(Puts his arms on her shoulders)* I mean it, Chris. If you want me to get them all in here and shout the truth from the housetops, I'll do it. If you want me to write Grandma Letty in Arabic, I'll do that, too.

CHRIS. I only want you to do that if *you* believe it's the right thing.

STAN. *(Crosses below CHRIS to the French windows)* I wanted to say something to people. I wanted to do really fine things with my writing. There are too many commercial authors— I wanted to be that one who is different, who helps people. I wanted to teach them to understand themselves.

CHRIS. Don't you see, darling, that's what you have done. You've done it through Grandma Letty. Haven't you noticed it happening in those letters you've been getting like the one from the stone-thrower's mother?

STAN. But, Chris, letters like those—

CHRIS. *(Crosses above sofa to STAN)* Laugh it off if you want to, but they're important just the same. You're helping those children. You're teaching them right from wrong, helping them in their formative

years. Anyone can tell *adults* what to do, but they won't pay attention—they think they know it all. It may be a bromide, but you can't teach an old dog new tricks, so what have you done? You've started teaching the old dogs when they're still puppies—while they're still young. Your philosophy shines through your books, darling, it's part of you and it's in whatever you write. You're training a new generation of Americans to think for themselves.
   (STAN *turns away.*)
—they'll pass it on to their children and their grandchildren. *(She turns* STAN, *holding onto both his hands with hers. She sits on the Left arm of the sofa)* You can't expect to change the whole order of things overnight, Stanley, it can't be done. Start at the bottom with the children—tell them what you think and believe. It may be through green snowmen and gruffy giraffes, I don't care, just as long as the seed is planted. It's only a small seed and it needs to be watered and taken care of, but we can do that. It's only a small dent in progress, but we can make that bigger, too. So, go on with your Grandma Letty books, Stanley—pour them out as fast as you can. Say what you have to say— I'll be with you doing what I can to help. *(Rises and crosses to the Center)* But if you kill Grandma, then you kill me, too, because you'll be a hypocrite and I don't respect hypocrites. You can't try to teach others to be honest and think for themselves if you're living a lie yourself. You've just started, Stan, and it's a long road. When we're finished, we'll have accomplished something. And, after all, that's the reason we're here, isn't it,—to make it a little better for the next generation? *(She takes a step towards him)* You ought to read your own books sometime and profit by the moral. Look at "The Green Snowman," Stanley—you'll see what I mean. *(She turns away)* Well, you asked for it—that's what I think. It's up to you now. They'll all be coming in soon: Prudence Harper wanting to complete a good story, Hoskins trying to protect book sales, Nora wondering what on

earth is going on. It's a tough choice—kill Grandma or give her a reprieve. You're the Judge and the jury—but, if she dies, I won't be here for the funeral. *(She goes up the stairs quietly.)*

(STAN *looks after her, sits on the sofa, takes a cigarette from his pocket and lights it. He takes a few puffs while he thinks over what she has said. He gets up, goes to the bookcase and takes out a copy of "The Green Snowman." As he thumbs through it, he crosses to the French windows. He is standing there when* PEGGY *comes downstairs.)*

PEGGY. Is everything all right?
STAN. Everything's topsy-turvey— I don't even know what kind of an author I am.
PEGGY. Brad thinks you're a great one.
STAN. Does he?
PEGGY. He read the story about the gruffy giraffe this afternoon. He said he sat in the children's section of the library and, if he liked the story under those conditions, it must be good.
STAN. I guess maybe it is.
PEGGY. He said it has a philosophy and a moral and, in its own way, is beautiful.
STAN. He said that?
PEGGY. And he ought to know—he's a genius.
STAN. *(Crosses above the sofa)* Peggy, do *you* think the stories are any good?
PEGGY. I love them, but don't go by what I say—I'm only normal.
STAN. It's the normal person's opinion I want.
PEGGY. Maude's sub-normal and she's read every one of them.
STAN. All of them?
PEGGY. Even the new one—the one you wrote under your own name.
STAN. When did she see that?

PEGGY. You left it down here one night and she took it to bed with her.

STAN. *(Crosses to the Center before he speaks)* What did she think of it?

PEGGY. To be frank, she said, "It stinks."

STAN. I sort of think she might be right. It probably does stink.

PEGGY. Don't pay any attention to Maude.

STAN. It's people like Maude that I have to pay attention to—the old dogs. You have to teach them when they're young. I never thought of it this way before but why do you go to school?

PEGGY. Because there's a law—why else?

STAN. *(Crosses in to sofa)* I mean, why do you go when you're young? Because that's the time you learn. That's when you form the thoughts and ideas which determine the type of citizen you'll become.

PEGGY. I suppose so.

STAN. That's what Chris meant. *(He looks at the book in his hands.)*

PEGGY. Is that the new Grandma Letty book?

STAN. Yes.

PEGGY. When did it come— I haven't seen it.

STAN. This morning. It's recommended reading for me. Chris said the plot was very apt.

PEGGY. What's it about?

STAN. Grandma meets a green snowman this time.

PEGGY. A green snowman?

STAN. Yes, he's green with envy because other snowmen are bigger or better dressed or better built than he is. Well, along comes a talent scout and signs our snowman to appear in the movies because he's so unusual. Off he goes to Hollywood pleased as Punch with himself because he's doing something other snowmen don't.

PEGGY. What happens?

STAN. They cast him in a movie right away and he gets more and more conceited, but there's one thing he hadn't counted on.

PEGGY. What's that?

STAN. *(Slows down his speech and is almost talking to himself as he realizes the point of his own book)* The first day on the set, they turn on the studio lights and they get hotter and hotter until the snowman melts away—all that is left is a small green puddle. Grandma explains to the other snowmen how wise they were to stay home entertaining little children and just being good snowmen. She says there are very few snowmen and they should feel proud that's what they are and take great care to accomplish their purpose or they'll end up useless green puddles, too.

PEGGY. That's nice, Stan.

STAN. Useless puddles? *(Slaps the book closed)* But not doing what they should have done—what they were meant to do! That's why Chris wanted me to read it. If I go on the way I'm headed, I'll be a useless puddle. Peggy, go upstairs and ask Chris to come down just once more. *(Starts to the French windows)* And get Maude in here, too, and the wig.

PEGGY. I hope you know what you're doing.

STAN. *(Turns)* I do. This green snowman isn't going to melt. *(He runs out.)*

PEGGY. *(Crosses to kitchen door and calls)* Maude.

MAUDE. What now? *(She enters.)*

PEGGY. I don't know. Stan told me to get you and Chris in here—and the wig. Then he went running out. He's over at Nora's.

MAUDE. Bringing the others back maybe. *(Crosses to French windows)* Let me look.

PEGGY. He went in all right.

MAUDE. What's he up to now?

PEGGY. Something. He sure was excited.

MAUDE. There he comes out again.

PEGGY. With the others. I'd better get Chris. *(She runs upstairs)* You wait here.

MAUDE. I wouldn't miss it. *(She crosses to kitchen door and waits.)*

STAN. *(Runs in)* Maude, I'm glad you're here.

MAUDE. If you think I'm doing any more acting, you've got another think coming.

STAN. *(Crosses to the foot of the stairs)* No—you've retired to the pots and pans.

MAUDE. I never realized before how much I loved every one of them.

PEGGY. *(Runs downstairs with the wig)* Here it is.

STAN. Thanks, Peggy. *(Takes the wig, puts it behind his back, as he crosses to above chair up Right.)*

PRUDENCE. *(Enters with CARL through French windows)*

   (PEGGY sits down Right.)

It's a good thing you called us— I was about to phone in half a story.

STAN. You'll get a full one now.

CARL. With pictures?

STAN. With pictures.

CARL. Good.

NORA. *(Enters through the French windows with a muchly paled HOSKINS who carries a cup of coffee in his hands. To CARL, who is standing in the way)* Out of the way.

HOSKINS. *(Weakly)* Where's a chair?

NORA. *(Guides him to the sofa where they both sit, NORA Right side)* This way, Mr. Hoskins—you'll feel better in no time.

HOSKINS. I only had one small drink.

CARL. Maybe we ought to get a picture of this.

PRUDENCE. *(Crosses to STAN)* He'll look worse in a minute. Stanley, let's get down to brass tacks. I get nervous sitting on a scoop.

NORA. As for me, I'm just plain curious what crime you've been keeping under cover.

STAN. You'd all better sit down.

   (PRUDENCE pulls out chair at phone table and sits with pad and pencil poised. CARL lounges on the back of the sofa.)

This will come as a shock to some of you. How do you feel, Mr. Hoskins?

HOSKINS. Better—now that I'm not standing.

STAN. Good. What I have to say starts a long time ago when I was just starting to write. I needed some money so I wrote a little children's story.

HOSKINS. You writing a children's story—that must have been good.

STAN. A publisher I know seemed to think so.

(CHRIS *comes down the stairs and listens to the rest of the scene.*)

He printed it and it sold so well that I wrote a whole series of such stories. The first one was called "Grandma Letty and the Hen Who Wouldn't Lay an Egg."

HOSKINS. "Grandma Letty and the Hen—"?

NORA. *You* wrote a Grandma Letty story?

STAN. All of them.

HOSKINS. But Grandma was—

STAN. Now we come to Exhibit "A." (*He pulls out the wig from behind his back.*)

NORA. Stanley Nichols!

HOSKINS. *(Half-rises)* That wig! What's this mean?

(CARL *sneaks down Left with his camera ready.* PRUDENCE *crosses to above the sofa.*)

STAN. It means that I am Grandma Letty.

HOSKINS. What? You?

CARL. *(Takes picture as* PRUDENCE *signals him)* Got it!

PRUDENCE. Good.

NORA. Why didn't you tell us?

PEGGY. He couldn't.

HOSKINS. You're Grandma Letty?—oh, no!

PRUDENCE. Poor Hoskie! *(As she helps him get the shaking cup of coffee to his lips.)*

HOSKINS. And this afternoon I—

NORA. *(To* STAN) You mean you've written all the Grandma Letty stories, Stanley?

STAN. Every last one.

NORA. But why did you keep it a secret?

ACT III MORE THAN MEETS THE EYE

STAN. Here's your human interest angle, Pru.

PRUDENCE. *(Sits on the Left arm of the sofa)* I'm writing.

STAN. When I sent in the first story, I thought it might attract more attention if written by a sweet, old woman. I must have been right— Hoskins published it. Then I kept up the disguise because I had some lofty ideas about writing a serious novel and didn't want to be connected with a juvenile series.

HOSKINS. But you were here in the room when Grandma came downstairs.

PRUDENCE. Couldn't you see through that, Hoskie?

HOSKINS. Were there two of them?

PRUDENCE. Are you going to confess, Maude?

MAUDE. I done it—great, wasn't I?

HOSKINS. Two Grandmas and now no Grandma!

MAUDE. They didn't recognize me when I played Topsy either. It was the middle of the second act before my mother knew I wasn't little Eva.

HOSKINS. I should never have come here. I'm ruined.

STAN. Don't worry—you'll go on getting your Grandma Letty stories if Pru is willing.

PRUDENCE. Me? What have I got to do with what you write?

STAN. You can ruin Grandma very easily. If you write up this story from a sensational angle, you can make me look so low that no one will ever buy another of the books. On the other hand, you can say I didn't want to disillusion the children by having them find out I was a young married man and I hope they'll forgive me—something like that.

PRUDENCE. *(Crosses to above sofa)* I don't know. It's a big story.

STAN. You'll have the scoop in announcing Grandma's change of sex and, if you play it right, I'll give you an exclusive on all of Grandma's future activities.

PRUDENCE. A permananet exclusive, huh?

CARL. On pictures, too?

STAN. Pictures, too.

CARL. *(Crosses to* PRUDENCE*)* How about it, boss?
PRUDENCE. It's a deal, Grandma.
(They shake hands.)
You must really love the little brats.
STAN. I do. I hope to have an even dozen.
CHRIS. *(From the stairs)* Then you'd better get started.
STAN. Chris, I'm glad you came down.
CHRIS. *(Crosses to Left of* STAN*)* I've been here for some time.

(They kiss.)

PEGGY. *(Crosses up Center)* Now that the adults are settled— I'm going over to Brad's.
STAN. Tell him I'll send him an autographed copy of "The Green Snowman."
PEGGY. He'll frame it. *(She goes out the front door.)*
STAN. What about it, Mr. Hoskins? Will you publish Grandma's books under a new author's name?
HOSKINS. This publicity, if handled right, will be great for book sales.
STAN. I thought you'd see the practical side.
HOSKINS. What about the plaque?
PRUDENCE. I'll start a tidal wave of public opinion in the magazines and newspapers. If Chris does her share, by this time next Spring, he'll be Father of the Year. What say, Chris?
STAN. What say, darling?
CHRIS. *(Smiles)* We'll see.
CARL. *(Still trying to do his job)* How about the picture?
PRUDENCE. Let's get at it. *(Crosses to chair down Right)* Stan, you be handing the plaque back to Hoskie. We'll caption it "Grandmother of the Year Declines Honor Due to Lack of Grandchildren."
HOSKINS. Great.
CARL. O.K. Stand over there. *(Indicating* STAN's *Left.)*

(PHONE rings.)

ACT III MORE THAN MEETS THE EYE

MAUDE. I'll get it.
PRUDENCE. Mrs. Nichols, you, too. Come on, Hoskie, on your feet.

(HOSKINS *gets the plaque and crosses to* STAN'S *Left.* CHRIS *crosses to his Right.*)

MAUDE. *(Into the phone)* Just a minute. *(To* STAN) There's a telegram for Grandma.
STAN. Wait a minute, Carl. *(Takes the phone from* MAUDE *who crosses up Left Center)* The first time I got a telegram today look at all that happened. *(Into phone)* Hello—this is Grandma Letty— Well, my voice is low—yes, read it, please— What? That's wonderful —Yes, take an answer. "Glad to come. Will fly West to discuss terms." Sign it "Grandma Letty."
CHRIS. What's all that about?
STAN. *(Crosses back into the room)* Another exclusive for you, Pru.
PRUDENCE. Shoot.
STAN. Walt Disney wants to film all of Grandma's stories.
CHRIS. *(Throws her arms around* STAN) Stan, that's wonderful.
STAN. We're going to fly out there and sign the contracts.
HOSKINS. Don't do a thing until I check the terms. I get a percentage, you know.
PEGGY. *(Runs in the French doors)* Stan! Stan!
STAN. What now?
PEGGY. Wait till I lock the door. *(She runs to the front door and locks it.)*
CHRIS. What's the matter?
PEGGY. It's Mr. Ellerbe. He's here!
HOSKINS. Lawton Ellerbe?
PRUDENCE. You mean the "Better Futures for Grandmothers" man?
PEGGY. That's the one. He asked me directions here. I sent him around the long way.

HOSKINS. He'll want to see Grandma. *(He looks at* STAN.)
STAN. Don't look at me. My dishonest days are over.
HOSKINS. Then you'll have to explain to him.
CARL. First the picture, huh?
STAN. How about you doing some explaining, Mr. Hoskins?
CHRIS. Yes, after all you get a percentage.
HOSKINS. But how can I—?
PRUDENCE. And I want that interview.
NORA. Let's all go back to my place and then I'll get the whole story from the beginning.
STAN. Good idea. Maude, you keep Hoskins here. After all, he started the whole thing by giving out my address.
MAUDE. I'll get the frying pan again if I have to.

(DOORBELL rings.)

STAN. There he is.
HOSKINS. Don't leave me.
MAUDE. Sit down. *(She pushes him onto the sofa.)*
HOSKINS. He has no right coming here without warning.
CHRIS. Well, you did. Now see how it feels.

(DOORBELL rings again.)

STAN. Come on everyone. Got your camera, Carl?
CARL. *(As he rushes out the French windows)* Right here.
NORA. Hurry up.

(She exits followed by PEGGY.)

ELLERBE. *(Off stage comes the voice of a man not unlike* MR. HOSKINS, *one who is determined to get his own way at all costs—someone who is used to speaking and having people jump)* Is anyone home?

ACT III MORE THAN MEETS THE EYE

STAN. *(Leading* CHRIS *to the French windows)* Come on, Chris.

HOSKINS. *(Starts to rise but* MAUDE *pushes him back)* Now, just a minute—

PRUDENCE. I'll be back to interview you and Ellerbe later. Don't let him get away, Maude.

MAUDE. I won't.

(PRUDENCE *goes out.*)

ELLERBE. *(Offstage. The front doorknob turns)* I hear voices!

STAN. Good luck, Mr. Hoskins. Tell the truth, be honest, and you'll be a good snowman, too.

(STAN *and* CHRIS *run out. BELL rings and pounding continues on the front door.*)

HOSKINS. Wait. I'm coming with you—
MAUDE. No, you're not. You're answering that door.
HOSKINS. But I can't—
MAUDE. If you don't, there are a few things we could tell Mr. Ellerbe.
ELLERBE. Did I hear my name? Open this door!
HOSKINS. What a mess!
ELLERBE. Open in the name of the "Better Futures for Grandmothers Foundation."
MAUDE. *(To* HOSKINS) Go ahead.
HOSKINS. All right. All right. *(He rises.)*

(MAUDE *gets between* HOSKINS *and the French windows to stop any final run of his.*)

ELLERBE. *(Off)* Do you hear me? *(Pounding continues.)*
MAUDE. Get going!
HOSKINS. *(Crosses to the front door)* Maude, we must all—

MAUDE. I know. Look pleasant—smile. *(She smiles broadly.)*

ELLERBE. *(Off)* If you don't open, I shall call the police. I shall—

(HOSKINS *unlocks and opens the door and for the second time that day, a complete stranger falls into the home of Grandma Letty.)*

HOSKINS. Do come in—

THE CURTAIN FALLS

MORE THAN MEETS THE EYE
PROPERTY PLOT
ACT ONE

Upstairs:
Pack of cigarettes with one left (Stan)

Off Right:
Dish towel (Maude)
Tray with 2 cups and saucers, cream and sugar, china coffee pot
Round tray with cup of coffee (Maude)
Mop, broom, dust-pan (Maude)

Off Left:
Pru's rose in buttonhole
Handkerchief (Hoskins)
Pillbox (Hoskins)
Small notebook (Brad)
Telegram in envelope sealed
Camera (Carl)
Plaque wrapped in brown paper and string (Hoskins)
Handkerchief (Brad)

On Stage:
Bookcase: small vase, center bottom shelf
knitting book, bottom shelf right
Mail box: (off Left) 15 unopened letters (1 business envelope) wrapped package containing 5 copies of "Grandma Letty and the Green Snowman"

Armchair up Right—knitting (start of sweater)
Telephone table: New package of typing paper, notebook and pencil
Coffee table: Ashtray, box of matches
Table down Right: Whiskey bottle (half-full); package of cigarettes, ashtray, box of matches

ACT TWO

Off Right:
2 glasses of water
Tray with 4 glasses of orange crush

Off Left:
Bunch of roses (Nora)

Upstairs:
Fan (Maude)
Knitting (Peggy)

ACT THREE

Upstairs:
Wig
Camera

Off Right:
Frying pan (large) (Maude)

Off Left:
Cup of coffee (Hoskins)

Strike:
Glasses and cups from table Right; take camera upstairs; clear coffee table except for the plaque, ashtray, matches; telegram from telephone table.

MORE THAN MEETS THE EYE
COSTUME PLOT

STANLEY: *slacks and a sport shirt changing to a suit during act one.*

CHRISTINE: *simple housedress changing to a smarter and more dressy outfit during act one.*

PEGGY: *Man's white shirt, rolled up dungarees, changing to skirt, sweater, and loafers during act one.*

CYRIL B. HOSKINS: *dark business suit with vest.*

PRUDENCE HARPER: *an attractive suit for act one; a smart and sophisticated dress for acts two and three.*

CARL HENDERSON: *a sport jacket and slacks with a loud tie. He always wears a hat.*

BRADLEY: *dark slacks with a light colored pullover sweater. A white shirt under the sweater, but no tie.*

MAUDE: *A light blue maid's work dress.*

NORA: *A simple, light colored dress that she wears when working around the house.*

MISS JENKINS: *A dark colored suit, extremely tailored and rather severe.*

LAWTON ELLERBE: *A dark suit with a conservative tie.*

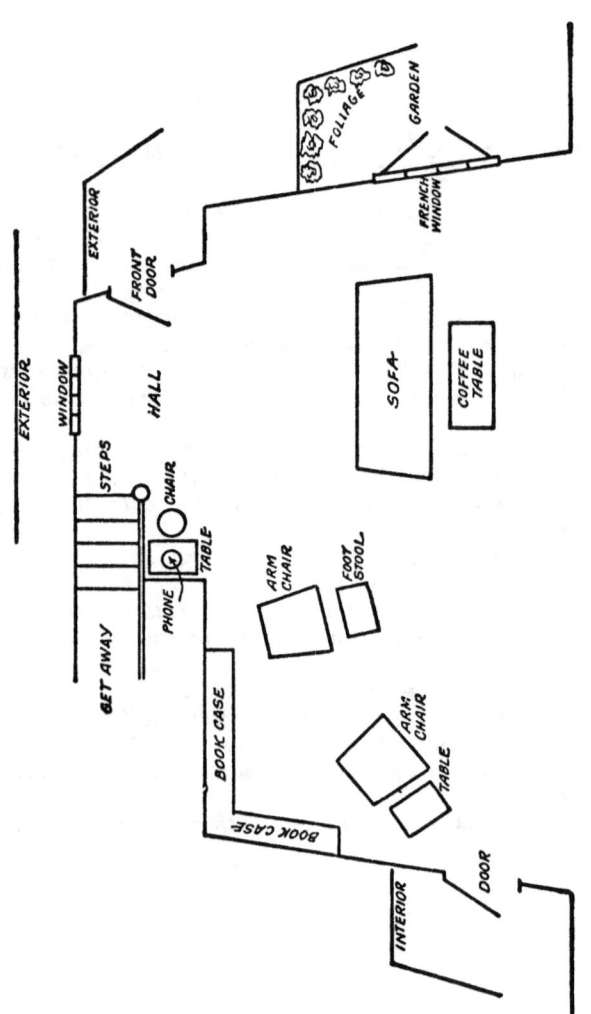

Also by
Fred Carmichael

All the Better To Kill You With
Any Number Can Die
Best Laid Plans, The
Coming Apart
Done To Death
Don't Mention My Name
Don't Step on My Footprint
Double In Diamonds
Dream World
Exit the Body
Exit Who?
Foiled by an Innocent Maid
Frankenstein 1930
Guess Who's Coming to Lunch?
He's Having a Baby
Hey, Naked Lady
Home Free
Hot Property
I Bet Your Life
Inside Lester
Last of the Class
Luxury Cruise

Meet My Husbands
Mixed Doubles
Murder is A Game
Murder on The Rerun
Night Is My Enemy, The
Out of Sight... Out of Murder
Over the Checkerboard
P is for Perfect
Pen Is Deadlier, The
Petey's Choice
Robin Hood Caper, The
Said the Spider to the Spy
So Nice Not to See You
Surprise!
Ten Nights in a Bar Room
Trouble with Trent, The
Turning Point, The
Victoria's House
What If?
Whatever Happened to Mrs Kong?
Who Needs a Waltz

SAMUELFRENCH.COM

NO SEX PLEASE, WE'RE BRITISH
Anthony Marriott and Alistair Foot

Farce / 7 m., 3 f. / Int.

A young bride who lives above a bank with her husband who is the assistant manager, innocently sends a mail order off for some Scandinavian glassware. What comes is Scandinavian pornography. The plot revolves around what is to be done with the veritable floods of pornography, photographs, books, films and eventually girls that threaten to engulf this happy couple. The matter is considerably complicated by the man's mother, his boss, a visiting bank inspector, a police superintendent and a muddled friend who does everything wrong in his reluctant efforts to set everything right, all of which works up to a hilarious ending of closed or slamming doors. This farce ran in London over eight years and also delighted Broadway audiences.

"Titillating and topical."
- "NBC TV"

"A really funny Broadway show."
- "ABC TV"

SAMUELFRENCH.COM

THREE MUSKETEERS
Ken Ludwig

All Groups / Adventure / 8m, 4f (doubling) / Unit sets
This adaptation is based on the timeless swashbuckler by Alexandre Dumas, a tale of heroism, treachery, close escapes and above all, honor. The story, set in 1625, begins with d'Artagnan who sets off for Paris in search of adventure. Along with d'Artagnan goes Sabine, his sister, the quintessential tomboy. Sent with d'Artagnan to attend a convent school in Paris, she poses as a young man – d'Artagnan's servant – and quickly becomes entangled in her brother's adventures. Soon after reaching Paris, d'Artagnan encounters the greatest heroes of the day, Athos, Porthos and Aramis, the famous musketeers; d'Artagnan joins forces with his heroes to defend the honor of the Queen of France. In so doing, he finds himself in opposition to the most dangerous man in Europe, Cardinal Richelieu. Even more deadly is the infamous Countess de Winter, known as Milady, who will stop at nothing to revenge herself on d'Artagnan – and Sabine – for their meddlesome behavior. Little does Milady know that the young girl she scorns, Sabine, will ultimately save the day.

SAMUELFRENCH.COM

www.ingramcontent.com/pod-product-compliance
Lightning Source LLC
Chambersburg PA
CBHW070644300426
44111CB00013B/2252